Eastenders
Don't
Cry

by

Joe Morgan

First published in the U.K. April 1994 by New Author Publications Ltd, South Woodham Ferrers. Tel/Fax: 0245-320462.

Printers: Redwood Books, Trowbridge, Wilts.

Cover Design: Joe Elgie

Typesetting: Statim Services, Billericay, Essex

ISBN 1 897780 95 8

Price in the U.K. £4.99

Index

Introduction

I woke up that Sunday morning with a tongue like sandpaper. Outside, the rain was teeming down. My head was swimming round, as it did so often after a Saturday night of too many drinks, too many mixed drinks. Being a character with a lot of friends meant being bought a lot of booze, and I just could never refuse the pleasure of good liquor and good company.

Having gingerly made my stocky way to the kitchen for some Anadins, I returned, heart thudding loudly, towards the bedroom. On the way I made a slight detour to the bathroom mirror, in the vain hope of trying to find what sort of creature had been sleeping in my mouth.

I got back under the warm covers, a soft sound from beside me made me turn; it was my wife, still asleep. I looked at her and remembered back to the slim, attractive girl I had first come across in Germany, just after the war. I mused on how times had changed, my mind slipping back to my East End childhood. I realised just how far I had come from that two-bedroomed slum tenement in Canning Town to this, my own property, here in a nice New Town.

Thinking of the early days caused my mind to wander down the meandering paths of hangover induced memories. I felt a twinge of sadness as I pictured my mother doing all the chores she had to do to bring up a huge family on next to nothing. She had died just a few years ago, and I still missed her. With her had gone a world that those who now enjoyed prosperity could not begin to imagine. I marvelled at how she managed, but at the time I had not given it a second thought.

If my father had been given a regular job, he would probably have lived a great deal longer than he did, but years of having to wait for back-breaking work at the dock gates, or shovelling coal down the gasworks, as he had done at sea as a lad, took their toll. What really did for him though was the munitions work he had to do in war time; it poisoned him and killed him, not quickly but gradually. Those in charge did not give a monkey's for the fate of men like my father, they did not care if the men worked for a pittance or rotted in the despair of unemployment.

None of this ever got my father down though. God! what a character he was. He drank hard and played hard, but that was the only way he could keep the anger and bitterness he must have felt under control. He was always the optimist, he would turn to me and say, 'No matter son, one day we'll have Socialism'.

I chuckled to myself at the thought. Perhaps one day we will have. I still repeat my father's hopes to my grandchildren. I fervently hope they will grow up in a world devoid of the humiliation of unemploy-

1

ment, the misery of wage-slavery, the high-handedness of public servants and the sick worship of anything materialistic above all else. In short, a world without the principles and values expounded by those vicious bastards — the Tories.

I lay in bed and felt anger and resentment rising at the thought of the way they had treated people in the 'thirties, and how they were getting away with it yet again. I have never made any excuse for my hatred for their ideas and methods, I will never apologise for my complete opposition to their way of life. It is precisely because of the passion that I brought into my politics that I was able to do well in that sphere. I was never a wishy-washy middle of the roader, prepared to endure them with a faint dislike but pathetic acceptance. My politics was fire and anger, and what ever anybody else may say, it worked for me and, for a time, the people of Basildon.

I have lived to see the dreams I had for the Basildon area perverted and shot to pieces by the stupidity, incompetence, narrow outlook, cowardice and sheer bloody-mindedness of both Labour and Tory councils. Both people I counted as enemy have messed things up.

I wanted Basildon to be the centre of a Thames region stretching from the outskirts of London to Southend. I wanted Basildon to be a town full of life and interest and industrial prosperity at its heart. Instead, today we have a town that is a byword for all that is worst about the culture of 'Essex Man'. A town centre that is deserted at night and decaying throughout the day. An area devoid of any really substantial industry and commerce.

I made mistakes when I was in power; that is true. My style did not allow anyone to sit on the fence when opinions were voiced on the subject of Joe Morgan. Either you hated 'The Godfather', or you loved 'Father Joe'. Yet whatever the case, people knew one thing about me, I was always true to what I believed to be in the best interests of Basildon, and I was always loyal to those I could address as 'comrade'.

Looking up at the bedroom ceiling that was what saddened me most. You expect the worst from those who openly oppose you, but it is the sly methods of those who are 'on your side' that always catch you out. Those who put their own ambitions before the needs of those they were supposed to serve betrayed the loyalty and comradeship that is meant to be the cornerstone of the Labour Party organisation. I was stupid enough to let them out-manoeuvre me, because I had one main failing, my loyalty to people who just did not deserve it. In the end, I laid a trap for myself, and walked into it. Even then, it was only because of connivance and cowardice that those who sought my downfall were able to gloat. But as I will show over the chapters of this book, it is me who has had the last laugh over the back-stabbers.

I though of how I had crossed swords with them all, the British Army and the Salvation Army, the Civil Service and the not so civil servants, prime ministers and cabinet ministers, headmasters and headmistresses, rogues and royalty. I am proud to say I upset them all, not just out of devilment, but because they were wrong.

I reached out for a bottle of drink that was on the bedside cabinet, taking a swig straight from the neck. Old habits die hard, but if my missus had seen me do it she would have killed me.

Then I remembered that my grandchildren would be coming round later. They loved to hear stories from grandad, especially the ones about Canning Town. Just now and again I would throw in the odd fairy tale, but they always knew, saying, 'That's not true', so it was back to the tales of the East End.

I had plenty of tales to tell, more had happened to me than most people in a dozen lifetimes. I looked at my wife. Her life story alone would make a film script: her existence in war-time Germany and her escape through Russian lines to be with me in the West.

Then she stirred, asking if I was asleep. When I told her I had a bit of a headache, she typically responded that it served me right. She had been my mainstay and support in all I had done in public life, she had always backed me, no matter what.

I began to wonder if anybody would believe all the things that had happened to me. Maybe it was about time to put the record straight. Films, television plays and books had barely scratched the surface of what life was really like for East End folk before the war. People who called themselves 'working class' had made fiction that bore little resemblance to the life of ordinary people.

It was also time I put the record straight about all the corruption and cheating I had come across, both that I had been able to stop, and that which proved too powerful for me to expose effectively.

Where would you start with such a life?

I had started off in the East End, and ended up here in this bungalow in Basildon, but the stops on the journey in between had been numerous: Berlin, Poole, Northern Ireland, the Isle of Man, Buckingham Palace, 'Lousy' Loughton, Paris, Whitehall and, most exotic of all, Aldgate, which was the Ends of the Earth to a cockney urchin such as me. I could start with one of the figures I had come across, Oswald Mosley, Harold Wilson, Dick Crossman, Keith Joseph, Tony Benn, the Duke of Edinburgh, but they were not the key to my life, just helps and hindrances, like some gigantic game of snakes and ladders. No, something else.

I suppose the best way to get people to understand why I though and felt the way I did would be to show them where I grew up: my London, warts and all.

Chapter One
NARROW STREETS AND
BROAD IMAGINATIONS

Everyone in the East End knew who we were. Wherever you went, people would point and say 'That's one of the Moggy Morgans'.

Moggy Morgan was my father, and in an area of larger than life characters he was one of the biggest and most colourful. We, his family, were just as big an colourful; fourteen kids our mother gave birth to.

I was born in Canning Town, the ninth of those fourteen, and named Joseph Edward.

The East End I came into had narrow streets with 'exotic' names: New Barn Street, Forty Acre Lane, Freemasons Road. Their names belied the slum dwellings and poverty that existed up and down their lengths. They were mean streets, but they were also my playground. In fact the whole East End was a playground for deprived kids who played at games that cost no money; old bicycle wheels became hoops and lamp posts were rope-swings; then there were marbles and hopscotch, top and whip, pitch and toss, conkers to crack and cigarette cards to swap. The grimy streets were alive with enjoyment.

In those streets at night we watched the gas lamps being lit by the Gas Lighter with his long stick that turned the gas jets on. We would watch the Lascars — seamen from the East Indies — walking back to their ships with goods they had bought at Rathbone Market. We were careful to keep our distance because we were sure they would kidnap us and sell us abroad.

In those streets people would sit outside on their front doorsteps. I vaguely remember my grandfather sitting out on our step carving at some wood. Then my grandmother would come out and give me sixpence to go to the 'Cherry Tree' off-licence, where I would buy her bottle of gin.

As children we would look up from our games to see our Uncle Alf marching down the street. Upright and fit, he had done a lot of boxing which meant you could almost see the pride bursting from inside him. He would grab me or my brother and order us to pull our socks up, whether we needed to or not.

My spinster aunt, Daisy, worked for the Jews in Aldgate — so we knew she must have money. Every week she gave each of us a penny. (Over fifty years later, when I visited her weekly in a residential home, she would secretively pull my hand towards her and give me ten pence, saying 'There you are my boy, buy some petrol for coming to see me'; I would solemnly thank her and slip the coin back into her apron pocket.)

Those streets really came alive on Saturday nights with all the parties and fights. Our people saw Saturday as the day of enjoyment, and enjoy it they did — even if it cost all that they had; and since they had little, it usually did.

The Second World War bombings and fires began the end of those streets and the end of the appalling poverty lodged inside them. Yet the end of those streets also meant the demise of what was good about the East End: the loyalty and the comradeship amongst the neighbours. Those streets are nearly all gone now. Some old customs still linger, some families still remain loyal to the old creeds. But in the place of those narrow streets concrete monstrosities have been created. Get-rich-quick speculators have cordoned off vast areas, killing what was left of the dock trade for the sake of Yuppy flats and a city airport. Even Labour councils have betrayed the East Enders and thrown their support behind the developers who are destroying the dock lands.

Even so, I will always remember the sense of security the narrow streets gave me; the sound of the children, the cockney humour, the cry of the muffin man, the hot chestnuts and the outings to Barking Park — to me at that time, a journey abroad. Above all else, I will always remember a mother and a father who were always there when I returned home. Our material existence was poor, but we Morgan children did not know we were poverty stricken — we had grown up with it; it was not unusual or remarkable. We only knew that our family gave us love, respect and loyalty.

As I grew up and left those narrow streets — ending up on the constantly dug up pavements of Basildon — I learnt how poor we had been. I could see how to change the situation for others — so I entered local politics.

The streets are quite broad in Basildon, but politically they are more narrow than Canning Town's ever were. The love, respect and loyalty of my childhood East End were replaced by the hate, derision and duplicity of modern Essex. However bad things were in my political life, however much the Tories tried to thwart my plans, however often my own party stabbed me in the back, I kept to the ideals and vision formed by what I saw and what I learnt on those childhood streets.

My father gave two advantages over most other local politicians — one was toughness — East Enders don't cry — the other was a fierce belief in the rights of the working class. My father was a communist by nature, although he was unaware of it. He voted Labour, but his own convictions were to the left of any of that party's ideas; he was for social revolution — yet he did not know he was a revolutionary. His own upbringing ensured that it could not have been any other way. People often say that I have a chip on my shoulder; if that is true then my father must have had a boulder on his.

Moggy Morgan was born at the end of the Victorian era. His mother could not afford to keep him, so he was sent to an orphanage. He ran away at one stage, but his mother's re-marriage after his father's death meant that she could take Moggy and his brothers and sisters away from the prison-like conditions.

At 11 Moggy earned his own crust by humping coal for a merchant, sleeping in the yard at nights. A year later he went on board a ship to work. He was the coal-trimmer, shovelling the fuel near enough to the boiler for the stoker to use it. If he put the coal down too far away or not quickly enough, the stoker would beat him up, striking as hard as he would have at a fully-grown man. Moggy was often knocked flying, until he was old enough and big enough to hit the stoker back.

During the First World War Moggy was torpedoed, left floating on an open boat for days. The injuries he received meant that the whole of the lower part of his jaw bone had to be removed.

After the War he went into the docks to work. The pay was 5/- a week, of which 1/- had to be given to the foreman to make sure that you were retained by him for the following Monday. When no work was available there, he would walk to Beckton gas works to shovel coal for the night.

During the Second World War, Moggy was diverted out of the docks to work in munitions at Woolwich Arsenal. As a result of handling chemicals all day, he would come home with all of his skin a terrible yellow colour. Most of it could be scrubbed off, but his hands were permanently tainted. Today it is accepted that this constant exposure to various chemicals caused cancer in many munitions workers.

The incompetence of British officialdom meant that he was re-directed back to the docks, but the damage had been done. In my opinion he was sent to Woolwich by mistake in the first place.

The ill effects the work had caused him were multiplied by the sever bronchial pneumonia that years of shovelling coal had resulted in. Each night Mum would wrap his chest in Thermogene wool, and put mustard over it to aid his breathing. I was about ten or eleven years old, when I remember hearing my father screaming — Mum had put too much mustard on; all the skin came off his chest as the wool was removed. There was blood all over him. We could not afford a doctor, so the wound had to heal on its own.

The constant bronchial coughing made his legs swell up too. He would get a terrible thirst, and have to drink bottles and bottles of lemon water that Mum made up for him.

For all his suffering, he was a cheerful, happy-go-lucky soul. Although he had a vicious hate of the Tories and seethed over the exploitation of ordinary folk, nothing else could draw the same venom from him. One day he would be broke, and the next he would have a good win on the horses or dogs; then he would give it to someone with a hard luck story or buy something absolutely extravagant. If there was anything left over he would gamble it away. Whatever he did he enjoyed it. He enjoyed as much as he could of a life that was to be relatively short.

I was closer to my father than the rest of my family; I probably knew him better than anyone. The words of advice he gave have stayed with me: 'Always remember this Son. Always make sure your family has food and a roof over their heads. No matter how you get the money, look after your family. And never trust solicitors, vicars, money lenders or the police. They're all against the ordinary Working-class.' Although I did not fully agree with the words, I used them as a guide throughout my life. I always knew that my own deeply held convictions came from Moggy's political views.

Yet to most people, my father was a good friend who loved a gamble and a pint. He had raised one of the largest families in the East End, and his attitude to life was to stop worrying about tomorrow. He lived for the day. His motto, often used — 'something will turn up for tomorrow, don't worry' — did not always come true though.

I cannot help but smile as I remember the times when I went to look for him, only to find that he was in a certain lady's house round the corner. He had a good life, the old man, where women were concerned.

I would help him with his other 'job', as a bookmaker's runner, at a time when off-course betting was illegal. Also I was the only one of the tribe who regularly accompanied Moggy to see West Ham play at home every other Saturday. Likewise he would smuggle me into the speedway; I would crouch down below his coat tails and shuffle under the turnstile. As I got older we would go to the dogs. I would put my own money on — perhaps a princely 2/- — and shout and scream as the dogs tore round the final bend. My father stayed calm, and would not say a word, yet he often had £5 riding on the back of his choice. Winning and losing came alike to him.

Once upon a time my father bought a car. He had won some money, the only way he could get hold of any large sums. He could not drive, he had no insurance and no road tax. None of this worried him, one of his mates could drive. Everyone in the family got into the car, though how we did, god knows; and we drove down to Southend. We stopped at every pub on the way there, and every pub on the way back. We kids loved this, because every time the car stopped, we got a packet of crisps or a glass of lemonade; it was an outing, Dad had won money, so Mum did not have to go to the pawn shop that weekend. As we had driven off I had told all my friends 'My Dad's become a millionaire and we're all going to live in a castle', though I suppose I knew that next week the money and the car would be gone. Mum would be back at the pawn shop. The car would go the same way as the pianos my father bought. He would bring home a nice piano, only for the old tally man with his horse and cart to come round and take it away a few weeks later, all the kids in the street running up the road after it.

With Moggy Morgan you never knew what he was going to do next. I had seen him walking along the street, leading a goose by the string round its neck. He had won it in a game of cards. He came walking along the street, the goose waddling behind him, everyone laughing. Mum said 'What you going to do with that goose?'. He replied that he was going to keep it till Christmas and then kill it. Everyone knew that in a couple of days he would probably lose the goose to someone else in another game of cards.

So that was my father; his character and presence held sway over all of us. Having been born in the 1880s, his attitudes to the family seem primitive now, but they worked. For instance: if I or any of my brothers fell out with each other, my father would dispense his own justice. The two who were arguing were taken out to the backyard. They were then made to fight it out with their fists until one hit the ground. The one left standing was right, so that was the end of the argument. This seemed very fair to me as a small boy. If I said that Don Bradman had scored a century in the last Test Match, and one of my brothers said no, then if my brother knocked me down I knew that he was right, I was wrong. It was the law of the jungle, it was not fair, but it prepared us for the harsh world outside.

As for your sisters, they were only there to serve we menfolk. Once you became a man, your sisters could not argue with you. When did you become a man? When at fourteen your father called you in, sat you down; he would give you a nut-brown cigarette to smoke and a pint of mild and bitter to drink. He would then say to you 'Now you're old enough to go and find yourself a woman' — you were a man. I suppose it is because of my father's attitude that I am still very much a male chauvinist today.

Why was he called Moggy? Well moggy is a Jewish term either for a gentile who works for Jews, or someone who has some Jewish blood in them; my father's grandmother was Jewish; both Moggy and his

8

sister worked for Jews — he was a runner for Barney Jacobs, the bookmaker, while Aunty Daisy cleaned for Jewish businessmen.

On Sunday mornings I would have to go across the road to one of my father's mates, where all the men would be sitting playing cards. It was my job to tell Moggy that his dinner was ready; normally I would not run errands, but I did not mind that one. I knew that when I went in, the men sitting around would let me have a drop of their beer, or give me a penny.

Moggy would come back home to our two-bedroomed down-stairs flat, where all the rest of the Moggy Morgans would be waiting; Mum, having prepared the food, my grandparents, then there was Liz, the eldest, who was given most tasks around the house; then my other older sisters Mill, Nell — the rebel, and Daisy, who always seemed to be out; so it was not too surprising when she eventually emigrated to New Zealand. Waiting at the table would be Bobby, the eldest son. He was a Billy Bunter figure, with Mum having to buy adult trousers for him, and then cut the legs down to make a good fit. He worked as a messenger boy, but would soon join my father at the docks. My next two brothers were complete contrasts: wild Alfie and quiet Harry. Alfie was always getting into scrapes, he was afraid of no- one; again, he would go on to work in the docks. 'Harry Boy' was a gentle creature loved by all the family. Then there was the bane of my life, my sister Ivy; she was always threatening to report me to our folks for creating havoc at clubs or with my mates. Of my four younger brothers and sisters squeezed into our kitchen-cum-living room Billy was the one who always followed me around. He would grow up to become a champion amateur boxer.

My sister Joyce was to have an unfortunate accident in which she lost her sight; she went on to attend a school for the blind. Then came the two babies, Pat, who would grow up to be a member of Peggy Farrell's Dance Troupe, and Bertie, the youngest, who would be another Morgan to work at the docks, before joining Newham Council to be a foreman.

So that was Moggy's tribe. He would make a fuss of all of us, tousling our hair and cuddling us before we would eat.

Mum, who was saddled with looking after all of us, was a different kind of person altogether. She would never show much affection to-wards any of her children; she was either unable to express her love or more likely, just too busy. I never stopped to think how she man-aged to cook, clean and provide for us all. My thoughts were always directed elsewhere.

Like all the kids in our street my toys were few, if any; my imagi-nation was fired by my surroundings. Canning Town was the world to me, if it lacked forests (for me to be Robin Hood) or deserts (Beau

Geste), then I could invent them. My friends and I knew little about the world beyond the East End, but our fertile imaginations more than filled the gaps in our collective knowledge.

My earliest memory is of bath nights — Fridays. We had a long, tin bath, which my mother filled up with water from the old copper that stood on the range. We kids went in by age, so it was often less than clean water that the young Joe was immersed in; the state of the water was always compensated for by the vigour of Mum's scrubbing. She would pour a bottle of carbolic into the bath and then scrub each child. As she washed us she would sing, usually Al Bowley's 'I'm looking for an angel'. Then it was up onto the big, old wooden table to be dried.

Mum was also a fund of knowledge and advice. It was she who would warn us about the Lascars, the Chinese and the Jews. Each racial community in the East End lived in ignorance of the others. As a result fear and mistrust grew up in the insular Cockneys, and my mother was no exception. Her ideas on other peoples became our ideas. So it followed that all the Jews were rich and spies on the working class. We did not know about the sweat shops where many of them slogged away for a pittance. In fact, as a whole, Jews were virtually banned from the West Ham area, and generally tolerated only from a distance. Our childish imaginations led us to think that they kept their gold and diamonds in the long beards the men wore. We would imagine cutting their beards off and dividing the spoils. Likewise then Sikhs in their turbans came round the doors trying to sell goods from their suitcases, we were tempted to rob them. We knew that the turbans would be full of gold and coins. If we knocked a turban off, the half- crowns would roll down the street where we could pick them up.

Mum would also warn us where not to go. You had to be careful near Limehouse, it was a foreign country. The Chinese who lived there smoked drugs and wanted to kidnap your sisters to sell them to China. We always skirted round Limehouse, and if we saw a Chinaman we would run before he could catch us and kill us. Ironically, the boot was really on the other foot concerning violence and slavery.

Even more ironical, the black people from Custom House were accepted as 'normal'. Because they and their families had lived in the area for generations, they had integrated into our way of life. We did not think of them as black. When in later years we talked of 'blacks', we were referring to the immigrants from the West Indies; so were the black people already living here — after all, they were merely dark-skinned Cockneys.

Even then my mother was able to explain their colour. The sun had burnt their skins black; we would have black skins if we went to

10

the country where they had first come from. As for their food — they ate poison, which would kill us; God made them so that they could eat poison. So they were tolerated by Mum. Even so, many years later, when she was aged 84, she would not be treated by a black nurse for her varicose veins. Nor would she eat the hospital 'poison'. To a black doctor she said 'You can't come near me, you just want to have your way with me'.

Mum was a figure of trust, so the day she dressed me, and took me down to school for the first time, I went along willingly. I was four and a half years old. Imagine my confusion then, as she left me screaming my head off, trapped inside this gaunt, terrible looking building — all grey brick and bars on the windows. She left me there in the corridor. 'You'll be coming home again, I'm not leaving you'. I just could not understand why my mother did not want me any more.

My fears at being left alone amongst strangers were to be well founded over the years: the ordinary schools of the 1930s were not temples to learning, but prisons where you learnt your place in life. They were not there to encourage thought, but to squeeze independence and questioning rebellion out of you. If your work was incorrect, you were not told where you had gone wrong by an understanding teacher, but belted for being stupid by a sadist.

I can remember most of my teachers as being very vicious. One of them (who incidentally owned a clothing shop as well) would take a fresh cane and prepare it as a weapon in front of the class; first he took out his penknife and split the length into six parts. Then the parts were hardened in a bottle of vinegar — all the better to cut your hand open with. He frequently caned us. I was thirteen years old when he tried to hit me once too often; I grabbed the cane from him — he was small and weedy — then I walked out of class. The next day Moggy came and lifted this teacher off his feet, and said 'Never touch my son again or I'll kill yer'. The whole class clapped; I was a hero.

But it was not just my father who had to administer justice; there lived a large woman two doors down from us, a typical charwoman type. She was either a widow or her husband had left her. Her child had been harshly disciplined, so she marched into the school and promptly knocked out the offending male teacher with a single punch.

Yet believe it or not, on the whole I enjoyed school. I was quite bright, and good at my lessons. Only the continual savage punishments made me anti-education. I never learnt as much at school as I could have done — our school just did not give you the opportunity.

Fortunately there was an opportunity given by membership of the local library. I joined and became an avid reader. For some kids it was reading comics under the bedclothes by torchlight; Joe Morgan used his torch to read books instead. All the time I was getting an excellent tuition on the streets too. There were no text books, only plenty of practical lessons.

The rest of the family were suspicious of education and academic achievement, so I got a lot of stick over my reading; they thought me a cissy. As far as my mother was concerned, the sooner I left school and started to bring a wage into the house, the better.

On top of her attitude was the determination of the teachers to break my spirit. I would not conform to their mindless regimentation, so I often got six or eight of the best. However, on one occasion I smiled after receiving six of the best of best from the headmaster, so I was duly dealt another six blows. On that occasion I thought it prudent to bawl a little. Normally I was determined not to show my feelings, otherwise they had won. Afterwards, alone in the dark, smelly school toilets I would often sob my heart out, then, by way of a small boys revenge, I would piss all over the walls. I could then go back to class with a smile on my face. At that stage I had not learnt that you cannot change a system by kicking it; instead you have to get inside, then beat the bastards at their own game.

The teachers did not break me, but my brother Harry was not so lucky. One day he fell down some stone steps, hurting his head. The following day Harry Boy was in class, and appeared to be dozing at his desk. The teacher meted out the usual subtle response, smacking him round the head. He was probably more surprised than anyone when Harry Boy sunk to the floor. He was taken to hospital where he died in Moggy's arms two days later. He was just ten years old. I was only eight, it left a lasting impression. Of course the teacher was exonerated. After all, it was only another East End kid, why worry? As Churchill said 'The East Enders are only dock rats'.

Harry Boy's funeral was held, funerals and weddings being those two events in East End life where people would scrape together whatever means they had to ensure that there was a 'good send off'. I will always remember how I was filled with awe by the hearses, horse-drawn by a black steed with a huge, black plume on its head. This was death face to face.

For weddings people would always somehow manage to hire a car, a really posh one. Cars were a real novelty to us when driven down the street. When my eldest sister, Liz, got married, I got so excited; but we had to pawn a lot to pay for it — well worth it though. Weddings were often huge events, because of the size of the families involved. Even today, at a recent wedding, my 'immediate family' added up to 250 people; at the reception we reckoned there were over 400 of our kith and kin.

The other events that brought everyone out of doors were the street parties. The main ones I can recall are those held for King George V's Silver Jubilee in 1935 and King George VI's coronation in May 1937. On both occasions it was the pawn shop to the rescue. We really knew how to enjoy ourselves, the pleasures were simple by today's standards, but were more than enough for us then.

For most families the pawn shop was a lifeline, even so, some just could not manage financially. That was when the Relieving Officer came round. He was an official, the inter-war years equivalent of the Social Security Department. If you applied for relief he would come to look at your worldly goods. If he found say, that there were five people in a family, but six chairs round the table, then that extra chair went up for sale. The amount of cash made from the sale of any such items that were not considered to be necessary would be deducted from any relief paid to you. The R.O. as he was known, was also responsible for dishing out school dinner coupons, vouchers for hob-nail boots for barefoot children, and tickets to allow you to visit the dentist or hospital. His word was law, he was God.

You could often be waiting at the dentist's or in the hospital with that precious ticket in your hand. Then the receptionist would enter the waiting room and ask 'Who can pay a shilling?'. If anybody could, they got priority to be treated. Those of us with relief tickets were kept to last, regardless of the nature of our ailments. It seems today that nothing has changed too much.

If the combination of the pawn shop and the R.O. failed, then there was only one thing for it — a moonlight flit. You could always tell which families would flee in the middle of the night with a loaded handcart and some battered suitcases. These were the folk who had 'decent' furniture and other nice things; they had no desire to lose their worldly goods to the R.O. or the landlord. If they were lucky they might find a different landlord and start afresh. If not, then eventually the goods would have to go, with the soup kitchens and hostels beckoning.

Traditionally, the big landlord round our way was the Bendebow family. In the Eighteenth Century the original Bendebow had built a lot of properties in the area to house the workers at his wharfs. He would look out of his window each working morning. By using his telescope he could see as far as the entrance to the docks. If any of his workers passed through the portals late he would find out who they were. They would then lose not only their job, but the house that went with it. Bendebow did very good business. By our time, if

13

you were a young couple about to get married, you would go to the current generation of Bendebow and ask to be housed. If either of you were the child of a current tenant, then a house or a flat was found for you to rent.

The local council had very few properties to offer by comparison. Even today Bendebow's agents, Scrutton, act as a large landlord who still house the sons of tenants.

All this meant that people used to stay in a closed and close community for generation after generation. Consequently, not only were we all largely ignorant of the rest of the country, we children knew next to nothing about the rest of our own city. To us, even nearby Aldgate was abroad. The Thomas family, who ran the local shop would cause us to snigger at their funny Welsh accents. The countryside round London was full of milk and honey — full of people living off the fat of the land; we knew this to be a fact. It was our duty, when we went to the country, to take the yokels' apples and milk off of them. We did not look at it as stealing, it was our East End kid's creed to outwit anybody who was not 'one of us' — to use someone else's phrase.

Of the other cities, the only one that we were aware of, was Glasgow. We knew that its people were poor and lived in slums. They were like Cockneys; we felt a bond with them.

Yet we knew all there was to know about the West End, at least, we thought we did. The West End was where the King and his family lived, at Buckingham Palace. We did not have a clue about places like Windsor Castle or Sandringham. We thought the Tower of London was that part of Buckingham Palace where the King locked up people he did not like, little realising it was a separate building only a short distance away, down by the river.

All the rich toffs lived in the West End too, everyone a millionaire. As boys, we could never fathom why we heard that a local shop or warehouse had been broken into; when we became grown-up (i.e. ten), we were going up the West End and break into all those posh jewellery shops, and steal diamonds worth thousands. Not for us robbing the poor corner shop. Alarms, grilles, the police, and other obstacles to our dreams either never entered our head or were a mere detail.

The other feature of the West End was that all the film stars — British and American — lived there. In fact, we knew Hollywood was up West too. It was like a version of Disneyland to us.

Films were our biggest escape and imaginative inspiration. Bert Tapman, a local bookie, would give all the kids a magic lantern show for a penny each during weekday evenings. For an hour we would sit enthralled at the bright images on the screen. Yet our desire for

14

fantasy and entertainment demanded better things — moving pictures. There were two places to go to see the 'flicks': the Apollo and the Addison, which was a real flea pit — literally. The foyer decorativeness and majesty of picture palaces were quite impressive for seven and eight year olds, but inside the auditorium it was a very different prospect. At the 'Addo' as you walked in, you were made to sit down on a plank- like seat; the usherette tried to squeeze as many of us as possible on, until the plank was chock full of little backsides. An attendant then came round squirting 'Flit', a choking spray designed to kill the fleas and bugs some kids had. Then the Saturday matinée would begin: Flash Gordon or Buck Rogers serials; Tom Mix Westerns. The Pathé News would give you glimpses of the real world beyond Canning Town.

As we got older we demanded shocks and gore. 'H' horror certificate films were for adults only. This was a minor problem for boys who were five-foot-nothing tall. We walked into the cinema with Woodbine cigarettes hanging from our lips. Hardly able to see over the kiosk counter, we casually replied when asked if we were over 16 years of age, 'Of course, can't yer see we're smoking?' Such was the ignorance and stupidity of the kiosk woman, that she said 'Oh yes...', and we were then allowed in, to sit terrified by the likes of Todd Slaughter in 'Murder at the red barn'.

A popular film of the time was 'Werewolf of London'; I went to see it when I was about 14. When I came out, thoroughly petrified, I looked up to see a full moon.... I ran all the way home from the cinema in Custom House, dived under the bedclothes and stayed well hidden.

Of course, we all wanted to imitate our big-screen idols — mine were John Garfield, Jimmy Cagney and George Raft. So if I was not playing the gangster, then I was pushing the girls about and giving them the occasional slap, just the way Garfield did to his leading ladies. When he made a film about the Merchant Navy, we boys put our jumpers on back to front to look like sailor's roll-necks. We would try, unsuccessfully, to break into empty places, thinking we were Jimmy Cagney.

Other entertainments were of course West Ham (if they were winning), and my real love — speedway. There used to be more than just conventional races down at the track. Often you would see novelty events such as a race between a speed cycle and a cheetah, with the cheetah winning.

Curiously enough, there was also a lot of excitement over the University Boat Race each year. You could not imagine a world farther away from those streets of ours than the rarified world of Oxford and Cambridge, but I suppose the two-horse race element

15

of Mortlake to Putney appealed. Cambridge always won — much to my annoyance. I always wore the Oxford ribbons which were sold for a ha'penny outside the cinemas which screened the race for tuppence.

Self made entertainment abounded as well. Our gang's peculiar enjoyment was to jump on a horse-drawn container van — usually the one belonging to the Cornhill company. 'Let's go on the Cornhill' we would say. This involved waiting on the corner of the street, jumping on the back of the van as it came past. Holding on to the outside of the container for dear life, we could not normally be seen by the driver. Other cart drivers would try to attract his attention to the fact that he had extra 'cargo' on board, which meant an attempted over the shoulder lash from his whip; often though, we went undetected until the van approached the Blackwall Tunnel, where it was then time to jump down and walk back home.

If we had been well off, we could have taken a tram ride back, but instead they remained just wonderful contraptions to look at as they rattled up and down the East End. In any case, I doubt if the conductor would have let such dirty little urchins on board.

So it was no surprise when all the kids were asked to come along and cheer the first journey of West Ham's new trolley bus none of us were allowed on it or near it. We were all bribed with a penny lollipop to line the inaugural route and cheer, as the Mayoress, Daisy Parsons, drove the bus along. We gazed at this huge, red, shiny piece of new technology in wonder. It was for us what a space-shuttle take-off is for modern children. Pictures were taken of Daisy Parsons at the wheel. We were all told to keep out of the way, being dirty, horrible little things who would spoil the propaganda of the council's brave new world. As the trolley bus started kids began to chase it, cheering, down the street, cheering after this lovely new machine with its electricity poles reaching into the sky. Daisy Parsons ignored us all, she was waving, but only to the press, she had got the pictures and the publicity she wanted. But we cheered anyway, this was a great adventure.

Afterwards my father remarked about our Labour Mayoress, 'She's a stuck-up cow who's betrayed the workers'. I did not understand what he meant at the time, but I was to find out all about West Ham Council and their principles first-hand several years later.

Canning Town was solid Labour, no surprise there. But there were a lot of other shades of political opinion around. Many young men were in the Communist Party, bitterly opposed to the spread of fascism and the deadly poverty of the Great Depression. Other people were those spreading the fascism, lured into its evil practices by its seemingly easy solutions to complicated problems; others admired it for the strength, the solidity and emphasis on patriotism and the family it preached. When the Spanish Civil War erupted, the local young men who went off to join the International Brigade to fight were looked on as heroes by the majority of East Enders. Yet when we boys saw newsreels of the German Condor Legion mercilessly dive-bombing Spanish towns and civilians, we could only marvel at the 'exciting' spectacle of these aircraft screaming down towards their targets, ruthlessly attacking innocents.

In fact, the political naivety and insularity of the East End came to the fore during the abdication crisis. To us, the loss of King Edward VIII because he wanted to marry an American commoner who was also a divorcée, was far more important than the events taking place in Spain. Mrs Simpson was even more hated than Hitler. People thought it was all an American plot to get rid of our King. We thought that the country would just disappear without the monarch. To us, the King was England, we had no concept of him as just a figurehead.

The kids would march up and down the streets singing'

'Hang, hang, hang Mrs Simpson,

Punch the old whore in the eye....'

When the King did abdicate, people were crying in the street. So then we punched holes in cans and set them alight using spirit, and began to sing,

'Mrs Simpson stole our King,

Chop her head off.'

Stanley Baldwin, the Prime Minister in the middle of all this, was just someone that my father would run down all the time. He was also the owner of a business, Richard Thomas, at Poplar. It was from there that Baldwin sold steel to Germany via Franco's Spain, right up until the outbreak of the Second World War. I was briefly directed to work at Richard Thomas during the War, testing metal jerrycans for leaks by submerging them in water.

Although many people saw the rise of international fascism as a threat to all of Europe, our only direct contact with it came when it threatened the hullabaloo that passed for peace in Canning Town.

Oswald Moseley was a knowledgeable and gifted man. He had been an M.P. in both the Labour and Tory parties, and, if he had waited, could have led either of them. His maverick streak meant that he became disenchanted with mainstream politics. Like many others, he thought the answer to Britain's troubles could only lie in the use of a more direct route than parliamentary democracy to achieve economic and social ends.

Inspired by the successes and glamour of Hitler and Mussolini, he formed the Blackshirts. Their stark appearance and vicious anti-

17

semitism earned them the hate of the greater part of the East End. Moseley and his thugs lay much of the blame for the country's ills on the Jews. He knew the existing distrust in areas like ours could be played upon. Some fell for it, others saw the error of their ways. Many young Jewish men joined the Communist Party as a direct result of Moseley and his politics. It seemed that the Communists were the only organization that would stand up to the Blackshirts.

Although the insularity, jealousy and distrust that existed in the East End was, at its worst, no better than Moseley's idea to rid Britain of its Jews, on the whole it had never amounted to anything like the hatred this man was preaching. His skilful oration had engendered sufficient support for his movement, but our natural left-wing leanings meant that we were definitely on the side of anyone Moseley saw as a threat. Moseley announced that he was going to march through the East End. The communists and the Cockney dockers were determined to stop him. There were running battles and barricades at places like Cable Street, but my part in all this, at ten years old, was to be a 'runner'.

The Blackshirts intended to drive into Canning Town in lorries. Then they would get out and begin to march. The men of Canning Town were waiting as a human barrier. To give advance warning of the lorries approaching, boys were positioned at intervals from Aldgate back to Canning Town. They were the 'runners' who would relay the advance of the enemy.

I was waiting on Canning Town Bridge, my goal being to run to the Beckton Arms pub with the news of the impending fascist invasion.

The lorries were sighted. When it was my turn to pass on the message I set off as fast as I could, shouting 'The Blackshirts are coming!' at the top of my voice. I doubt that the distance was even a thousand yards, but to me it seemed like an Olympic marathon; I had done my duty.

The lorries turned up and the Blackshirts spilled out. The Communists and dockers set on them immediately. As if from nowhere, a horde of policemen descended on the battle, trying to defend the Blackshirts. Truncheons were used left, right and centre to cosh those opposed to Moseley. The man himself travelled in a car, his whip in his hand. But it was Moseley who was whipped, his face scarred for life by someone in the crowd who struck him as he tried to get out of the car.

Eventually the Blackshirts had had enough; even the police could not save them. Oswald Moseley never came to the East End again.

My only other 'political' experience of the time came when I helped to hand out leaflets to campaign against the Conservative candidate for the council. I went about shouting a slanderous rhyme as I gave the leaflets out, it had a familiar ring about it....

'If it wasn't for the King,
We'd do the old prostitute in!'

That was me at ten years old. I thought I knew it all. I was cocky, crafty and rude. But then, so were the rest of my gang.

For years a story had been going round Canning Town about a house which stood alone and empty. Folks from round about claimed that of a night, there was the sound of a wooden leg coming down the stairs of the house. Some adults were terrified, and would not go near. Children on the way home from play would glance nervously at the house, and then run past. 'Hopping leg's coming, hopping leg's coming', they would scream as they dashed past in terror. We kids soon had a nickname for the place — haunted hoppy leg.

One cold, bleak afternoon in late November, when I was ten, I sat with my cronies, the usual gang that roamed those streets. I was the leader; then there was Charlie Kent, whose father left home while Charlie was only a few weeks old. There were six other brothers and sisters in the Kent family. They were exceptionally poor, even by the standards of Canning Town in the 'thirties. As a result, Charlie went about in a ragged pair of trousers, with no shoes on his feet. To complete the picture, his nose was always running. Charlie was very loyal to me.

Ron Williams was entirely different. His father had a job, which meant the family were well off; they even went on holidays. Because of this, Ron was never really accepted by the rest of the gang. He was always trying to prove that he should be made the leader. As a result I had quite a few punch-ups with him. He might have been a better fighter, but I was dirtier, so I always won.

As an antidote to our arguing there was Tom. Tom was for peace; when arguments and rows occurred it was always Tom who would say, 'Well, come on, we're all mates, let's go somewhere'.

So it was that Tom had said that morning, 'Let's say we find a lorry and go up to Poplar'. And we had done that, and then walked back, stealing a few chocolate bars from Larkin's sweet stall along the way. While we were munching this afternoon feast Ron turned to me: 'I bet you couldn't go to the haunted house on your own'.

'Who couldn't? I'm not scared.'

'Not much you ain't.'

'You shut your mouth, otherwise I'll fill it full of teeth.'

Even at this early age we were using the language that we had heard our elder brothers and parents using. 'I'm not scared of going,' I said. 'I'll go anytime; I'll even go when it's dark.'

19

In saying this I knew that Ron's parents, being little different from others in our street, would not let him stay out when darkness fell. My cunning had dictated that there was no way Ron could know whether I had been or not.

'All right,' Ron replied. 'We'll make it tonight.'

'Sure.'

With that we decided to go in for something to eat. I walked into our room, where as usual Mum was at the sink, washing clothes. 'Where have you been? I wanted you to run some errands for me. Young Harry Boy has had to go again.'

'Why me?' I asked truculently. 'I'm not running no bloody errands.'

'You watch your language my boy. No good will come of you; everybody says that. Your grandparents say it as well.'

I strolled into the bedroom I shared with the other thirteen. There was just a partition between the two rooms. I looked around t see if there were any toys lying about; to me a toy was any piece of wood carved out to the shape of a bat. Nothing there. One of my brothers had got it and gone over to the park. I went back to the kitchen. 'Is there anything to eat?' Mum cut me a thick knob of bread, spreading it thinly with jam. 'Ain't you got nothing else to eat?' 'No we haven't. You know your father's not at work, and look at the state of those shoes you took off on Sunday. Also my boy, I've been told that the penny you was given to put in the church box, you spent.'

'No I did not.'

'Yes you did, your sister told me.'

I was not prepared to argue, so I walked out of the house. This was quickly becoming my defence against others, I would just walk away and leave them.

The day drew on, starting to get a bit darker. I stood with my mates, my back against the wall of Thomas's shop. Every night we stood there, working out elaborate plans. Plans about how we were going to break into the shop and steal a lot of food. And all the money in the till. (We had set our sights a bit lower by now, realising that the Crown Jewels were a bit out of our grasp.) 'There must be two pounds in there at least,' we used to say to each other. 'One day we'll break in there.' Most of the time was spent waiting for little Peggy Thomas, the prettiest girl in the street, to come out. Everyone had their eyes on her.

As darkness closed, much to my surprise, Ron came walking up the street. 'Well,' said Ron. 'Are we going up to the haunted hoppy leg?' I was surprised and dismayed. I gulped, 'Sure, come on then.' We started to walk through Granville Road, a turning off of Fife

Road, where we lived. My steps became slower and slower. I started to make excuses: 'Here, look at these railings, let's climb up and balance on them.'

'No,' said Charlie. 'I'm not doing that. You know Georgie Spinks? He done that last week and the spike went through his leg. Yeah, and he had to go to hospital. He had all stitches; someone said they cut his dick off as well.'

'They wouldn't do that. How can they do that?' asked Tom.

'Well they did. I heard my mum talking about it to my dad.'

'You haven't got a dad, you bleedin' liar,' I said.

'Well I call him my dad. It's some man my mum met. He's going to be my dad.' The rest of us looked at each other, sly grins on our faces. We all knew about the men who wanted to be Charlie's dad. We had heard our parents talking about it.

Gradually we came up to the house and stopped. Although it was not completely dark, it was gloomy enough to be eerie. To everyone's surprise, there was no one else about; it was too early for men to be coming and going from the pubs. This only made matters worse. 'Well,' said Ron. 'In you go, bighead.'

'When I come out of here, if there is a leg, I'm going to hit you right across the bleedin' head with it. That'll shut your mouth for good.'

I knew there was no way out, the others were all looking at me. This was more than just a dare to go on. 'That cunning bleeder Ron's engineered this,' I thought. 'He's going to show me up so I can't be gang leader any more; I've got to go in.'

I walked in. The house was full of dirt, broken bits of furniture lying around all over the floor. The windows were all broken, and the front door had been smashed open a long while ago. The older boys had been in and nicked all the lead out of the plumbing, probably the roof too. An eerie silence filled the whole house. 'I'm in, can you hear me?'

'You haven't gone upstairs yet, where the haunted hoppy leg is,' came the faint answer back. From the front room I had moved to the kitchen. The place seemed like a mansion. I had never seen the inside of a house with an upstairs as well. Even the faint light left by the setting sun had gone, and it was now quite dark and still. Slowly, I climbed the stairs, my heart thumping like mad. I kept looking back, terrified of the slightest shadow. 'I wish I'd kept my mouth shut, all I should have done was beat Ron up; that would have solved all the problems,' I mused. 'Just beating someone up.'

At the top of the stairs were two rooms. 'Sod it. That door would have to be closed.' I was looking at the entrance to the front room — the bet was that I had to go to the window there and show myself

21

to the rest of the gang. I pushed the door to the other room open.
I did not even look in, but quickly stepped back. Turning, I entered
the front room, it was empty, just an empty dark room. At the window I looked down on the others in the gloomy street below. I'd won
the bet. Haunted house? There was nothing here. 'I know why that
is, it's because ghosts don't come out till midnight. The others don't
know that though, I've beaten them.'

For a fleeting moment I felt very brave, I was not scared. Then,
as I turned from the window there was a noise. Bang! Bang! Bang! I
could feel the blood drain from my cheeks, and if it had been possible, my hair standing up on end. 'It's the leg, it's coming up after
me.' I wanted to run but I could not move. It was as though I was
nailed fast to the floor. I felt I was going to suffocate. Bang! Bang!
Bang! The noise went on. Then, like a spring let go, I ran blindly
through the door. Virtually falling down the stairs, I stumbled out
into the street.

The rest of the gang, seeing me running, started to run themselves. They did not know why, but they ran and ran, like mad, with
me following. At last, completely out of breath, I had to stop and put
my head between my knees, forcing air back into my lungs. After a
few minutes the gang stopped running, and came back to where I
was crouching.

'What happened Joe?' they asked. 'What happened?'

'It came after me. It's there, the hoppy leg is in there. It's true,
there really is a hoppy leg.'

The rest of the boys looked at me in amazement. 'You actually
saw it?'

'Saw it? I had to fight it. It attacked me so I grabbed and threw it
in the corner of the room. Then, when I came down the stairs, it
came after me and tripped me up. But then I picked it up and threw
it back up the stairs. Then I ran out here.' I could not help getting
carried away with the story. The others looked as me in awe, completely taken in by it all. I knew once again that I had proved myself.
I was their true leader.

My ability to tell the difference between the fact and fiction improved over the years, and my ambitions became less fanciful than
stealing gold and jewels. Yet even armed with the desire to tell and
seek out the truth, and improve the lot of other people, I could not
have achieved anything but for the gutsy, street-wise ten year old who
has stayed inside me from that day to this.

Chapter Two
INNOCENTS ABROAD

The summer holidays had arrived. I was roaming around with my mates, all only too glad to be away from school. To us, ahead lay six long weeks of adventure.

'We'll go over to Beckton Road Park,' I said to the gang. 'And we'll stay out all night, find some potatoes and bake them. Let's go up the shop and nick some eggs, and we can fry 'em.'

'What we gonna do for a tent?' asked Charlie.

'Oh, we'll make some sacks up, we'll find some sacks and make a tent.'

'Where you gonna find sacks from?' Tom this time.

'When the coal blokes comes round let's nick some sacks off the back of his horse and cart.'

'Yeah, but he hit a kid with his whip last time,' chipped in Charlie. 'He hit him with a whip you know, right across his back. Had to have an operation.'

'How come you're always makin' up bleedin' stories Charlie, about operations? First it was your mate who had his dick cut off when he fell on a railing, now it's a bloke hit with a whip.'

'Well that's what I heard.'

'Well you know what I heard?' Ron Williams joining in. 'I heard the Sally Army's giving tickets to go to Lousy Loughton: "Come to Lousy Loughton." '

It was always known as Lousy Loughton in Canning Town. We did not really know why, but there was a good reason. The Salvation Army would pack the children, little captive souls, onto a bus with an open top-deck. So tight was everyone seated that every kid who was not already infested with fleas soon was. It was always assumed that the fleas had come from the countryside in Loughton, so that is how this unfair description came about.

'Shall we go then?' I asked.

'I don't know,' Tom replied. 'We'll have to pray and all that shit, won't we?' Already our attitude towards religion, the State, in fact anything that smacked of establishment, was starting to form. 'It doesn't matter about prayin', we just go and sing a few songs and say a few prayers, then we get our tickets to go on the bus. Then they give us a bun and some cocoa.' That clinched it.

We went to a place called Bradley Street, which was only just round the corner from us. The Salvation Army hall lay on the junction of Bradley Street and Beckton Road. Inside the gaunt building children filled the wooden benches. Satisfied that no more could be squeezed in, a Salvation Army officer came to the front and announced that there would now be a few songs and a prayer: then a few more songs, and then we would all get a bun and some cocoa. No surprises there.

Whilst the buns and cocoa were prepared Charlie kept nudging me. 'Look, there's your sister Nell.' Sure enough, there she was, no uniform, but a Sally Army bonnet on her head. 'What you doin' with a Sally Army hat on Nell?' I shouted. Nell walked over, 'Don't be saucy, you, and keep quiet.'

'I'm going to tell Mum when I get home, she'll do her nut, you being in the Sally Army.'

'Mind yer own business.'

Nell was quite a rebel, always getting into rows at home. At 17 she was of an age where she wanted her own way. Although my father was quite easy going with we boys, he was very strict in what he would allow our sisters to get up to.

'And if you muck around in here Joey, I'll give you a clip, I'm tellin' yer, you behave yerself in here.'

'Ain't yer goin' to have a tambourine?' I taunted, and then started singing: 'Come and join us, come and join us....'

Everyone around began to laugh as a red-faced Nell stalked away.

Then the singing started for real. One of the favourite hymns was 'My cup is full and running over'. All the kids in the hall had to cup their hands together and say that they were as happy as could be, because their cups were full and running over. Yet most of these kids were in truth either at starvation level or close to it. Very few of them had shoes on their feet, not one of them had any decent clothes, but their cup was, apparently, full and running over. This mockery was lost on us at the time, but in the years that followed it would further shape our ideas, making us very cynical about religion.

After the singing it was prayers, more singing, and then, best of all, bun, cocoa and ticket to Loughton. As we left the hall we were told, 'Don't forget, and were reminded of the day the bus would be leaving on. 'Anyone without a ticket won't be allowed to go.'

When I got home, the place was packed with Morgans. It was always a battle as to who would get into bed first, as I slept with all my other brothers under the same sheets. I was already shrewd enough to know that in winter it paid to get in the middle, where the other bodies kept you warm. In summer you had to be quick, dashing into bed first enabled you to sleep up against the wall, where you would remain cool whilst your brothers lay in the sticky heat, some at the top, some the other way round, with their feet by your head.

I thought about Loughton before I dropped off. I thought I knew what the countryside was really like: in my mind it was a place where everyone was well fed, and everyone was rich. I did not know that the average farm labourer was as poor as any London docker.

The great day arrived, I met Tom and Ron out on the street. We started to walk up to the top of the road, and then into Beckton Road. On the way, Charlie came out of his house with his small brother. 'I'm taking him with me.'

'But he hasn't got a ticket Charlie.'

'Doesn't matter, we'll get him on.'

'Can't you know.' Then Ron said, 'Well my mate's coming, I'm going to get him on.'

'How are you going to do that?' I asked. 'Well,' Charlie interrupted. 'Someone told me that what you do, you get onto the bus and throw your ticket down. Then they catch it and use it to get on.'

'Well we can try it.'

I felt good as I swaggered along the street. Mum had not pawned my boots that week, knowing that I would need them for Loughton. They were new boots too. I looked reasonably smart as I got on the bus. 'Show me your ticket,' said a very official looking man. So we aired our precious tickets before running up the stairs to the open top-deck.

We wanted to sit at the front, so that we could see everything going on. The front seats were already taken. I looked at the boys who had taken them, and they were pretty big. 'Sod that,' I thought. 'I ain't taking them on, we'll have to sit somewhere else.'

'Come on, if we can't sit at the front, let's sit right at the back. There were already two or three boys sitting in the back seats. 'Off you get,' I ordered. 'These are our seats.'

'No they ain't, we was here first.'

'Look, we 'ad these seats booked and we 'ad to go out to get some sweets. Now get out.' The young boys look half frightened, undecided whether to go or not. They sat tight. With that, I got hold of a couple of their fingers, and bent them backwards. They screamed with pain, then hurriedly got up. Turning from halfway down the aisle, one of them said, 'You wait till our big brothers come on this bus, they'll learn you a lesson'. I knew that there were no big brothers, I could afford to be cocky; I made as if to get up, they ran quick enough then.

Looking down, we could see Charlie's brother and Ron's mate standing in the road. We dropped two tickets down to them. Sure enough, in a short while they came up to join us.

By now the bus was packed solid. Obviously far more kids had turned up than had been given tickets. A very irate man came up to our seat and said, 'Some of you boys haven't got your tickets'. For some reason he did not check his suspicions out. He continued: 'If I find out who it is, you'll all get chucked off, the whole lot of you. There'll be no trip to Loughton for any of you'. Then he left us alone.

The bus started, we were on our way. As we sped through the East End and out into Essex, we stopped our singing, gasping in amazement at the flat, green fields and nice houses that slipped by — it was a different world from ours. We were all looking forward to arriving in Loughton. Once off the bus it was going to be lemonade, sandwiches and running wild. Already we were making plans about what to do if we saw any cows — tie their tails together. Boys who had been on the trip previously starter to tell hair-raising tales of enormous cows that would chase and butt you; we city kids could not readily distinguish between cows and bulls.

Then we reached Loughton, all clambering off the bus into a big field where a huge marquee had been put up. First off were the organised games — rounders and my favourite, British bulldog. Having expended my energy on games, I thought to head off afterwards and do some exploring. The rest of my gang came along.

On the far side of the field was a fast-running stream. It was about five yards wide, with steep banks and a row of concrete blocks as stepping stones across it. Ron bet that I could not walk across the wet stones. 'Let me see you do it first.' Ron agreed, and crossed over the stream quite easily; his plimsolls had given him a good purchase. I stepped confidently onto the first block, tuning to pull a rude face at Ron as I did so. Before I knew what was happening my new boots slipped on the green slime that covered the concrete. I fell into the water. It was far colder and deeper than I had expected. Surprise, rather than fear was my reaction, until I realised that I could not swim. I started to yell for help.

By this time someone had run back towards the marquee for help. One of the Salvation Army men appeared with a couple of towels. He knotted them together and threw one end to me. By sheer fluke I caught the towel first time. I was hauled out, terrified and sopping wet. I had no underpants on (we never knew what they were), so my rough calico trousers were plastered to my legs. Worse still, boots, my nice new boots, the boots the Relieving Officer had doled out to my mother, the boots that were supposed to last three to four years, were sodden and ruined.

As I stood naked, wrapped only in a towel in front of friends, my only thoughts were that I would get the strap from my father. Not just because I had ruined new boots, but mainly because Mum would not be able to pawn them on Monday morning. That money might be the difference between eating and not eating. I fervently hoped

26

those boots would dry out.

It was a hot day, and a bonfire had been built in the middle of the field. The trousers were draped in front of the fire, and quite soon they were drier. Not dry, but wearable. So I continued with the serious business of joining in the games. I had bare feet and a damp backside, but I did not mind. Tea time was due, so all of us had to line up for our share. First there were a few prayers, which we all mumbled through as quickly as possible.

Looking back now, I often wonder why the Salvation Army bothered. Did they really believe that they were finding lost souls, converting anyone? Ninety percent of those kids at that outing had more street sense than the Sally Army officers ever would; we all knew the score, we were not going to be converted. We listened, nodded, did as we were told. For all the singing and praying, at the back of our minds the thoughts came through: 'Shut up you stupid bastards, when are you going to give us that tea and that bun?'. These officers professed to be christians, but they had precious little love and understanding for us. Rather than forcing religion down our throats, they could have tried treating us with some compassion and dignity; perhaps that would have had more effect. The way we were treated at that camp was not a lot different from the way our elder brothers and fathers were treated at work, if they had any. We were all just so much scum from the slums to be exploited.

Eventually it was time to leave Lousy Loughton. I went over to the marquee to get my boots, but I could not find them. I went to the adults to ask if they had seen them, but to no avail. 'All we can do,' I said to the gang, 'Is keep a look out as the boys get on the bus. They've obviously been nicked'. I decided there and then that if I caught the cowson who had taken my boots I would break his neck. We got on the bus, having not seen anyone with the boots.

I was very quiet on the journey back. The others shouted and cheered, I just sat, dreading going home. The trip home did not seem to be half as long as the one out. Suddenly we were back in London. The nearer to Canning Town the bus got, the more worried I became.

The bus pulled up in Bradley Street and we all got off. I walked away, dejectedly. My feet were hurting now. One of the officers grabbed me by the arm as I hobbled past. 'Here's your boots.' 'Where were they?' The officer said that he had kept them all the time, as he had heard me using filthy language. This was the punishment. I stood looking at him. Then I brought myself up to my full four foot, and looked him square in the eye, 'You bastard.'

'I'm going to get a policeman onto you,' he threatened. I did not answer. I grabbed my boots from him, but I did not run off.

Instead I sat on the kerb and defiantly put my boots on. Then I got up and looked over to the officer again. 'If I told my dad about this, he'd come and punch your bleedin' head in mate, Salvation Army or not Salvation Bloody Army. You can stick you bloody bus and your cups of cocoa up your arse, 'cause I ain't coming up there again.'

'If he had said another word I would have given him a right hook,' I told the gang, who could not credit how I had spoken to an adult. Proud as a cock sparrow, I started home. Mum was there to greet me. 'Have a nice day boy?'

'Not bad.'

'Get into any trouble?'

'No, but I fell over though, and there was this great big puddle. I got my trousers wet, and my boots, but I couldn't help it Mum.'

'Oh that's alright boy, it'll soon dry off. Did you hurt yourself?'

'No, it was only a puddle. Don't know how it got there, it hadn't been raining, but it was a big puddle.'

'Don't matter, take your good things off and go and put your old clothes. Then you can go out. But only for half an hour, no more.'

'No, I don't fancy going out, I think I'll stay in now and then I'll go to bed. Have you got a bit of bread and dripping?'

'Here's a ha'penny, go over to Wiseberg's. Go and get a bag of crackling.'

Wiseberg was the Jewish shop-keeper. He had two shops, Angell's the hairdressers with the fish and chip shop across the road, and another fish and chip shop next door to our flat. It used to stink the house out when they cured the kippers.

So I did as I was told. On the way out of the shop, two friends were waiting, so as usual I let them dip their fingers into the bag. So there we stood, three East End urchins, crunching away on crackling, the fat running down our fingers, down the sides of our mouths and across our chins. God knows what it did to our arteries, but some days it was all that we had to eat.

So the Sally Ann never did save me for Jesus. They did not save Nell either, she left after a few weeks, doubtless looking for something else to upset my father with.

Any sort of outings were few and far between. I was lucky enough, when very young, to be taken for a day out by my godparents, Mr and Mrs Crush. I cannot remember much about it, except that it was to Vange, ironically now part of Basildon. I know that I was not very old, because I could barely see over the long grass.

I did have one other holiday, one Easter, when Ron Williams' parents took me on holiday. Again, this was to Vange. Mr Williams had a job on the railways, so he was a rich man to us. Like many people at that time, he had what was called a 'Champagne plot'. These were small packets of land that could be bought for £100. When you bought your own piece of Essex you received a bottle of champagne. In this way little wooden villages sprung up in the countryside, as people built their own timber bungalows.

I had one last excursion to the outside world before Hitler's war turned all our lives upside down. The memories of that last year that I went hop-picking in Kent, before the war became too pressing, are as vivid now as ever.

Hopping, down in Kent. The whole East End used to wait for the hopping season to start at the end of summer. Most families went to the same hop fields each year, and more often than not the rest of your street would be working alongside you in the same field. We always used to go to Goudhurst.

The excitement would mount as the time drew near. Then when the day dawned, I could not wait for the lorry that would take us down to Kent. Each lorry would have three, four, or even five families, their chairs, their luggage and their cooking utensils all piled in the back. Then a procession would start from Canning Town, through the Blackwall Tunnel, past Poplar and out into the Kent countryside. At some 20 miles an hour it could take three or four hours before the hop fields were reached. All the way down we would be singing all the old songs. As soon as I hear those tunes now I am immediately sitting on the back of a lorry again.

We would arrive at a farm, where we were allocated a little tin hut to live in. There was not a lot of privacy, with only a thin partition between each hut, s that you could always hear what was going on next door.

My first job was always to go out with my brothers and sisters to collect twigs, dozens and dozens of them, which would make the base of our bed. We would lay all the twigs out carefully on the hut floor. Then Mum would press, squeeze and kneel on them until they were pliable. Straw was placed on top of these, and finally a blanket was thrown on top.

We all slept there together. There were not many men present during the week, especially later, when the war started. Some of them would come down at the weekends. There were one or two younger men — 'Fly boys' — deserters from the forces or those who had dodged the call-up. Their job would be to lift the giant hop bags onto carts. Then they would take the carts to the kilns, where the hops were dried out. The resulting dry hops would be sold to the brewers.

I was quite strong for my age, so I would often be given the job of pole puller: after the women had pulled the hops down from the wires they grew along, there would still be some hops obstinately stuck on the vine. My task was to get my hook underneath the vine and pull it, with its hops, down for picking. I was kept busy all day by the women doing the picking. They would shout out 'pole puller', and I would rush over to pull the head of hops down for them, blushing at all the sly jokes and remarks directed at me. 'Oy, ain't he a big boy? Wonder what he'll be like in four or five years? Then you can come and visit me with your pole any time.'

Although I thought I knew it all, I was still very shy near women, especially when teased like that. I would mumble about them being dirty old cows as I went from hop bin to hop bin. 'When's your older brother, Alfie, coming down?' They would ask, as Alfie had quite a reputation with the women. He was in the Navy by now, in a Special Operations unit.

When work was over for the day, I would wander off with my mates. We normally ended up either scrumping or sitting outside a pub with the adults. Some nights though, it was just sitting round the fire, often getting into scraps with one another. Most of the girls had to be in by eight or nine o'clock, so the boys would try to sort out one or two girls to talk to before bedtime. Sometimes it was rather more than talking; we would only cuddle or touch, but to us it felt as though we had just had sex. We would boast to each other as to how far we had gone with a girl.

After all the others had gone to bed, my little gang would be abroad, looking for, and usually finding adventure. The farmer whose land we were on had made it known that anybody caught scrumping fruit or stealing chickens would be sent home straight away, along with the rest of their family. Well, this proved to be too much of a challenge to ignore. If we came across a chicken we would coax it into a corner with some feed, catch it, wring its neck, and take it home for our mothers to cook. If we caught more than one then we would sell it to a family that did not have any thieving little boys to do their foraging for them. If we were not chasing chickens, then we indulged in that other popular rural pursuit, throwing stones at cows.

When we sat outside the pub in the evening, it was invariably to see if we could take part in another rural pursuit, namely being peeping toms. Sometimes one of the more flighty women would be picked up by a local man. We would all nudge each other, saying, 'Let's follow where they go.' The couple would nearly always end up by having sex. We would watch from what we judged to be a safe distance, our eyes growing as big as saucers. This is how I learned about sex, the wrong way, but it was exciting, which was all that mattered to us thirteen year olds.

One night we had our eyes on a women we knew. She had a big

mouth, so she was always easy to spot in a crowd. Having met a soldier in the pub, she led him off to a field near our huts. We followed. The lustful pair lay down in the long grass. We crept nearer, and nearer still. Somehow, one of us made too much noise. The soldier jumped up, demanding to know who was there. 'Sod this,' I said. The next thing we knew, all of us were in full flight. 'You little bastards,' shouted the woman, I know who you are.' I turned back to yell: ' 'Ere, you dirty old boot, we know who you are and we know what you're doing. You wait till your old man comes down the weekend, we'll bleeding' tell 'im.' With that we ran off again.

When I came back to our hut that night, Mum immediately questioned me: 'Where you bin?'

'Oh, just wandering around.'

' 'Ere my boy, you mind your own business about adults. I've heard something about you, what you bin up to?'

'I ain't been up to nothing, it's them dirty old boots.'

'Not so much of the old boots. You don't know what you're saying. She was just being friendly.'

'Yeah, I know what their being friendly was.'

'You watch it my boy, you've got too much of it for someone your age.'

I walked sulkily out into the dark night. Loads of people were sitting round their fire, talking and gossiping, some of them singing. 'Come on my boy,' said Mum. 'It's time for bed. It's gone ten o'clock.'

'It's too early.'

'It's not too early, now you come to bed.'

'I'm not coming to bed and you can piss off.'

'You wait till your father comes down, he'll give you such a good hiding.'

Mum was still calling after me as I wandered away. Obviously none of the other boys could sleep that night, because I soon came across the rest of the gang. It was Ron who had an idea as to what to do first. 'I was told that, of a night time, chickens are hypnotised. They just sit there, or stand there, and they can't move 'cos it's dark. All you do, you go and pick 'em up, put 'em in a bag, and you can get hundreds and hundreds of 'em.'

'I never heard of that,' I queried.

'Yeah,' said Charlie, 'I've heard that as well. Let's do it tonight, shall we?' I agreed. 'Let's go over the hop field and empty a sack out.'

'But them sacks are too big,' Charlie protested.

'That don't matter, don't matter how big it is, we'll fill it right up and sell chickens to everyone down here.'

'If we get caught we won't 'arf be in trouble,' said Ron. 'Why don't we take just half a dozen?

'Why? If they're all sitting there hypnotised, we might as well take the bleedin' lot.'

So off we went with a sack, scared to death, but even more scared to admit it. The moon was not out that night. Being London boys, we were not used to this pitch darkness. As we skirted past the farm we saw the chicken runs.

'Are you sure they'll stay quiet when they're in the sack? Ron asked, having doubts now.

'Course,' I replied, 'Stands to reason.' It was Ron's idea, but I was suddenly an Expert.

'What d'ya mean, stands to bleedin' reason?' Ron still doubted.

'First, they're hypnotised in the dark; well, it'll be darker still in the sack, so they stay hypnotised, don't they?'

We got closer, and I told the others that we would have to crawl across the last field to avoid being seen. 'Well say there's all cow shit in the field and it gets all over our clothes?' Charlie moaned. 'Look, we'll have to go into the Army before this war's over, then you'll have more than cow shit to worry about. We'll make out we're in the Army now.' So we crawled across the field.

As we got to the first of the runs I said, 'I can't find out where the gate is.'

'Well there's wire there — tie the wire round,' offered Charlie. Slowly I put my hand over the wire. Just then there was a tremendous noise from the chicken runs. It was as though every chicken in Kent had started to squawk at once. We froze where we were. A light went on in the farm house. Not for the first time, my imagination got the better of me. 'There's the farmer, he's got a gun, he'll shoot us.'

As we blindly stumbled over the rough turf, I though my lungs would burst. We did not know in which direction we were going, as we clambered over fences and scrambled under hedges. We could run no more. As we gasped for breath we looked black. All we could see was the blackness. 'You and your bleedin' hypnosis,' I growled to Ron. 'How can they be hypnotised if they make that bleedin' noise?'

'Well, someone must have shone a light.'

'No-one shone a light, it was your stupid story.'

'No it's not, I heard it, my dad told me,' this time Charlie interrupting. 'You ain't got a bleedin' dad, I told you that before. Your dad told ya. Where are we now? We're lost. My mum'll kill me. All we can do is to go back to where we ran from, then we'll be heading back towards the farm. We can't stay out all night.'

'Hang on, I know what I'll do,' said Ron. 'I'll climb a tree and see if I can see any of the camp fires.'

'That's a clever idea. How comes you never thought of that Joe?' Charlie asked.

'You're supposed to be gang leader.'

'I would of thought about it in a couple of minutes. My mind was working out how to get you all home, that's why I didn't think of it straight away. You shut your mouth, or I'll poke ya.' Ron found a tree and climbed into its lower branches. 'I can see fires.' So we stumbled towards them over the wet fields. We tripped over mole hills and slipped in cow pats. We arrived at the huts, scratched, dirty and truly miserable.

I went into my hut, telling the others, 'I'm going straight in. I'm not like you lot, I'm a pole puller. I've got to get up early.' Inside, the usual question from Mum, 'Where you bin?'

'Why? I've only been out five minutes.'

'No you haven't, it's half past eleven my boy, and you're in trouble when your father comes.'

I took my shoes off and went straight to bed. 'You taking your clothes off Joey?'

'Yeah,' I lied. 'No he hasn't Mum, he stinks,' one of my brothers piped up.

'You shut your mouth.'

'No, you shut your mouth.'

'Shut both your mouths up and get to sleep.' Within seconds, as usual, I was soundly sleeping.

Another day in the fields came round. By now I had learnt all the dodges. I knew that if I stayed to help load bags when the pickers had finished in the late afternoon, that there would often be a quarter bag left over. I would hide that bag. Next morning I would pour its contents into Mum's bin, so she would start off with an extra three or four bushels of hops that we would be paid for.

Work finished at about half three so that the women could go and cook a meal. They lit fires outside the huts, standing around cooking and gossiping, just as they might back in the East End.

It was while Mum was cooking for us that I joined the gang in a search for an old, deserted house that stood in the middle of the fields. We were going to break in, because there was gold inside. I told the others that all country people were rich, not like us: they got all their money from selling the hops. Then they would put all this money into boxes, or buy gold with it. The boxes of cash or gold would then be buried under the floorboards of their houses, so that ordinary folk like us could not get at it. I knew all this for sure. We would have to get a sack to put the gold in.

'You're always asking for sacks,' said Charlie. 'Can't you think of anything else but bleedin' sacks? Everytime we go anywhere you want to take a sack along.'

33

'What we going to carry it in then? You've got holes in your pockets — so that's no good.'

'Well we'll find something when we get there,' said Ron. He was by far the most sensible of us, but he never had ideas as exciting as mine. I hoped that there would be ghosts in the house, then they could grab hold of Ron and frighten the life out of him.

We found the house, it was huge and covered in ivy, even the windows. To an adult it would have been obvious that it had long been derelict, but we did not know that. 'How we going to get in if all the windows and doors are barred up? asked Charlie. 'Have to find something to break 'em open with,' I reasoned. We searched the ground around the house, but could not find an opening or anything with which to force our way in. I decided that we would need some tools from the huts. Since nobody would go back on their own, we all traipsed across the fields, occasionally running in short bursts.

It was on our way back for tools that we saw an aerial dog-fight going on. 'Look at that.' I cried, 'The 'ole sky's full of 'em.' This was not like London, with bombs raining down, so we foolishly stood there, thinking we were completely safe. We lay on the ground to watch. Once plane seemed to come down in flames no more than three or four fields away. I was excited. 'If we find out where it's gone down we might get some shrapnel and bullets and things.' We completely forgot about the house. This was more fun, we did not think that the plane could possibly blow up, taking us with it.

Sure enough, we found the plane a few fields away, engulfed in flames. We sat down cross-legged on the grass. We just looked. After what seemed like a couple of hours, we got up and walked over to the now burnt-out wreck. 'There might be a German in there,' Charlie suggested. 'What would we do then?'

'We'd have to go and fetch the Home Guard,' I told him. 'I heard that on the wireless.' As we talked, we heard noises. Four or five soldiers were coming over the field. As they drew nearer, a sergeant told us to clear off. 'We was here before you,' I argued, 'So why should we clear off?'

'Less of your cheek son, or you'll get a clip round the ear.' Ron butted in, 'Yeah? And you'll get one from my dad when he comes down.'

'Yeah, and one from my dad,' I added. The soldiers grinned and called us saucy bastards. One of them asked where we came from in London, our accents giving us away. I told him.

'Oh,' he said, 'I come from Poplar.'

'Cor, do you? You goin' to kill that German if he's in the plane?'

'Oh I don't think he'll be in there son.'

'Will you kill him if he is?'

'No, we'll take him prisoner.'

'Where will you take him?'

'There's a prisoner of war camp about four miles down the road, near Goudhurst. All locked up, they are.

'Can we take some shrapnel?'

'No,' said the sergeant. 'You leave things alone.' As the soldiers walked off, satisfied the plane was safe, the one from Poplar turned to us and said, 'Go and get yourself some shrapnel if you want lads, but be careful and don't hurt yourselves.' He winked, then turned away. We picked up some bits of metal, not realising that some parts would be quite valuable. To us it was all shrapnel; shrapnel we could tell people had come from a German aircraft

Back at the huts we swelled with pride and importance as we told everyone the details of the crash. To the young girls we were heroes, and the way we described events, we might almost have shot the plane down ourselves.

That evening the derelict house was remembered: 'Shall we go tonight?' suggested Ron. 'No, I'm not going there at night time,' I said. 'Why? Are you scared?'

'No, I ain't scared. I'm just not going of a night time. Anyway, it's too late to go now, we'd have to go over all the mud.'

'Nah, it's not the mud, you're just frightened.

'All right, we'll go.'

We turned to the girls who were sitting with us round the fire. Did they want to come along? They did not. 'Come on,' I cajoled, 'We'll be back before it's time to go to bed.'

'No, we'll come with you tomorrow.'

'Come with us now. Come on, it's Friday night, so your dads will all be down; they'll all go up the pub till ten o'clock, so we'll be alright.' Then came what I thought to be the clincher. 'Tell you what, you come with us and we'll give you these bits of shrapnel.' They did not want shrapnel, for some reason. Plan 'B': 'Ah, but we know where the parachute is, it's all silk, and you can make stockings out of silk.' The girls sat up and looked interested. 'You know where the parachute is?'

'Yeah, we 'id it, didn't we?' I looked at Ron and Charlie. They caught on and agreed, yes, we had hidden the parachute.

We set off for the old house again, this time with the girls in tow. We also had some tools — well, a screwdriver and a bit of metal. Now it was getting dark. The girls were nervous. They whined that we boys should go on, alone, after all, nobody in the group had a torch. We ignored them.

The house came into view. Ron and Charlie went over to pull the wooden shutter off of the windows. The glass was already smashed. I told the girls to wait whilst we climbed in to get the front door open. Inside was gloomy, but there was enough light to see that the place was completely empty. The front door would not open. We called to the girls from our entry window, telling them that they would have to climb in. 'We're not coming in there.'

'All right, you wait outside for us.'

Charlie, seeing that the place was empty, wanted to leave. Ron and I wanted to have a good look round. We walked through into a large room where there was a staircase. Fortunately, Ron said we shouldn't climb it in case it collapsed. Relieved, I agreed. We then found a kitchen with just a sink, single tap and table.

There were cupboards underneath the sink, but by now it was too dark to see if anything was in them. I suggested that it would be better to look for the gold during daylight. So we climbed back out of the window. I muttered to the others, 'Leave this to me with the girls.'

I went up to the prettiest of the girls, Marjorie. I knew her from back home, and I liked her. 'Full o' jewels in there. Couldn't get them out though; got to have a special light.'

'Why?'

'Because you 'ave, because there's all broken glass there, and you could cut your hand. And I'm going to give you some of the jewels.'

'Are you.'

'Yeah. Now let's have a little sit down 'ere and have a rest, shall we?

'No, we'd better get back to the huts, it's getting dark.'

'Well I thought we'd try and find a road, then we'll ask someone the way to the pub, and we can go and see if our mums and dads are there.'

'All right, we'll do that then.'

'But let's sit down here first. I've got all those jewels for you, and the silk parachute.'

'I'm too scared to sit down here.'

'It's all right,' I grinned, 'I'm with you.' all of us sat down on the grass, the boys getting hot with excitement and the girls giggling. None of us had ever had sex, although we boys thought we had. I started fumbling with Marge. 'Oy, leave off,' she said, pushing my hands away. 'You'd better let me Marge, or else I'm going to leave you 'ere. I didn't tell you before, but there's ghosts in that house, and monsters.' I fully expected her to swoon into my arms, terrified. Instead, she jumped up, and with the other girls chasing after her, ran screaming across the meadow. 'Don't go, it's alright. I was only joking...you're going the wrong way.'

36

The girls stopped, we boys caught up with them. 'You bloody fool Joe, saying that to them. He was only pulling your leg,' Ron explained.

'You rotton sod,' Marge rounded on me 'I'm telling my mum what you tried to do to me.'

'I didn't do anything — you wouldn't let me.'

'Yeah, but you tried.'

'I'm sorry Marge, come on, we'll go up to the pub.'

'No, we're going back to the huts.' Then Marge walked off.

The other girls though, thought differently: they started to follow us. I turned to watch Marge. She was walking very slowly. 'You go on, I'll catch you up,' I told the other four. I ran after Marge. 'I'm sorry, come on, come up the pub.'

'Alright, but I'm going to the hut first.'

We arrived back at the huts and sat down together on a log by the fire. Marge was still trembling, so I put my arm round her. She pushed me away at first, but soon we were kissing and cuddling. Then she whispered, 'Not here, someone might see us. I'll go and see if my mum's gone, then we can go into the hut.' The coast was clear, so I was beckoned over. We sat on the bed and started kissing. With eager excitement I then lay on the bed with Marge. My hands wandered over her body. It seemed that nature was about to take control when a little voice shouted out, 'Wait till Mum comes home, I'll tell here what you two are doing.' We both leapt up, only to see Marge's younger sister staring at us. I dashed out, stopped by the fire, and looked back. Marge was having a go at her sister. Then she started whispering to her. Whatever blackmail it was that she threatened, it seemed to work. Marge walked over to me. 'It's alright, let's go down the pub.'

We felt very close as we walked up the lane. It was as though we had actually made love. My thoughts were now preoccupied with getting Marge on her own again.

At the pub all the women were there with their husbands. Everyone was laughing and drinking: the war, their own poverty and worries of raising families temporarily forgotten. The latest Vera Lynn hits and some old cockney songs rose into the night air. Parents would come out of the bar with great big penny biscuits for their kids to eat. They were as solid as concrete, taking hours to munch. As I looked inside the pub window at all the happy faces, all I could think was, 'I'll be glad when I'm old enough to get drunk, won't it be smashing. Life seemed just about perfect.

All this was shattered when we came back to the huts. Marge came up to me, crying, saying that her father had received his call-up papers, so she had to go back home with the rest of the family. The next morning everyone turned out to say goodbye to Marge and her family. Her father had brought a friend of his who had an old car, somehow they all managed to pile into it. By now, saying goodbye to friends and loved ones was commonplace, but people cried just the same as they waved Marge's family on their way. The car chugged off, Marge's face looking back at me through the dusty rear window. I never saw that face for another twenty years.

I was sitting in a pub with my wife when Marge walked in with a man by her side — her husband. At the sight of her the memories of hop picking flooded back. I did not say anything. I just smiled as I wondered what might have been. But that was the past.

Shortly after Marge left, the hop picking season came to an end. As the lorry took us back through the lush, green fields towards London, I was unaware of the future. I would not go hop picking again. The war had altered everything for all of us. Maybe that was what fate had intended anyway.

By the time we were back in the East End it was dark and raining. The nightly air raid had begun. The sky was full of bombs and shrapnel. We took bomber raids in our stride now — the Luftwaffe wasn't going to panic us. We unloaded our things from the lorry quite calmly. Soon Mum was at the stove making hot cups of cocoa for the family. Another hop picking year was over.

Chapter Three
IT'S A LOVELY DAY TOMORROW

It was the 3rd of September, 1939. Mr Hitler had invaded Poland two days previously. Neville Chamberlain had just announced to the world that as a result Britain was at war with Germany. Soon everybody's life was going to be turned upside down. This war would prove to be a revolution for the working class of this country, although it did not seem, like it at the time: the Tories had got us into an avoidable conflict, and would eventually pay dearly for it in the 1945 'khaki' election. Even Churchill's war leadership would not be able to save them.

On a personal level, I would grow from street urchin to man in one step, robbed of my adolescence, like countless of others, by the demands of Total War.

During that last peacetime August everyone had been getting kitted out with gas masks, and there was talk of all the children having to be evacuated from the city. I was oblivious to what this would all really mean. My only thoughts were 'A war with Germany? That's funny, my dad was in the last war against Germany and now we're going at them again.'

I decided to ask my father what it was all about. I quizzed him when he came home the next night. 'Well, we're going to fight the Germans, the fascists. Fascists are against the working class,' he explained.

'Oh, I thought it was the Tories who were against us, that's what you've always told me.'

'Oh no. Now there's going to be a war we're all going to be together. We've all got to stick together to fight the Germans.

'What was it like to fight the Germans, Dad?'

It was a question I had already asked a hundred times. My father would tell me about being torpedoed, and how ill he became as a result. I used to delight in putting my fingers into the gap in his face where his jaw bone had been removed. He would make out that he was asleep as I did this, suddenly 'waking up' and playfully biting my fingers.

At first the War did not seem to make much of a difference to any of us: during the 'Phoney War' I would still go to school, still go down to West Ham speedway' Eric Riticitti and Bluey Stephenson were my idols — even now, the smell of diesel instantly reminds me of those nights down by the trackside. Moggy would still have a bet on where a fly buzzing round the room would settle next, or just about any other result that was open to chance. He was still so popular that people said if Royalty were to come to the East End, and someone was talking to Moggy, they would rather stay talking to him than go and look at the regal visitor. War or no War, if Moggy had some money he would still lend it to you, down to his last penny. Mum would still give him some stick for it too. So apart from British movie stars appearing on our screens and across the papers in uniform, very little changed in those autumn and winter months of 1939.

I had started to attend West Ham Municipal College from the age of 13. However, the mixture of mickey-taking at school (my accent was very pronounced and noticeable, even to the other Londoners in the class), ribbings about the official uniform (which I hated), or rather my appearance in it, from my brothers and sisters, constant nagging from Mum to go out and get a job, allied to a sheer lack of cash in the family to pay towards my learning, meant that I would leave school far too early for my own good.

But the prospect of leaving was in the future when it was announced that school would be closed for the meantime, the first real effect Hitler had on my life. Then Moggy told the family that he thought it best if we younger children were evacuated to the countryside.

I ended up being sent to Portland, in Dorset, along with my younger brother Billy. The first woman we were billeted on was a disaster. She was cruel and vicious. In her mind, she was taking in wicked, heathen little East Enders as God's work. She did not enjoy having us in her house, so this soon became obvious to us. We hated her.

One day Billy could not eat his dinner. Our holy lady made him open his mouth, as she tried to force the food down his throat. He vomited, nearly choking on it. That was enough for me. I jumped up from my chair and lunged towards the woman, kicking her hard in the shin. 'You dirty old cow!' I bawled. She of course had never heard that sort of language in her life.

'I'm going to report you to the Billeting Officer,' our red faced and furious landlady threatened. 'You do what you bloody like. I'm telling my mum what you did to Billy, and she'll come and hit you right in the fucking mouth, you bastard.'

That was the last straw. Rather than wait until the next day, she was going to see the Billeting Officer straight away. She tore out of the house to go and tell him that we would have to leave — today.

Things turned out for the better. The next woman we were visited upon was very good to us. She lived in Euston Square in Portland. Although she was still doing her religious duty by taking us in — she was a member of my favourite Christian organisation, the Salvation Army — we both liked her and her treatment of us.

40

Our time at Portland was marred by an untimely death. We had spent the day, Billy, myself and some other evacuees, in a disused quarry. We were playing and generally messing about until it was time to go back t our digs. As we set off, a cry came from behind us in the quarry. We dashed back to find one of our mates, Bernard, lying crushed under an enormous stone. He had stayed behind on his own, the stone falling on him with an instantly fatal result.

We were all very distressed and extremely sad at the time, but being young we quickly put this dark episode out of our thoughts in the weeks that followed. It wasn't long before we were out spending our days roaming over the cliffs, or chasing the goats that grazed along them. We would scramble down to the shoreline, where hours were used up in pursuit of crabs in the rock pools, patrolling the beach and just paddling in the waves.

I do not know which civil servant decided that Portland would be a safe place to send children to, but whoever it was must rank alongside the idiot who had my father directed from the docks to munitions, and then back to the docks again. Perhaps it was the same person, but I doubt it, the civil service spawns stupidity. Portland was a large naval base. If the Luftwaffe could get past Fighter Command, it was going to be an obvious bombing target. They did and it was.

Embarrassed officials hurriedly transported all of us kids back to London whilst they tried to find a genuine backwater to send us to. Mum had other ideas. She was fed up with evacuation. 'They're staying at home with us.'

The city I returned to was so different from the one I had left. With the schools closed, the atmosphere seemed weird, even our old childhood haunts were out of place in some way. The blackouts led to unsafe streets as crime soared in the enforce darkness. Jumped-up A.R.P. wardens strutted around, telling people to put lights out in no uncertain terms. Folk ignored their pompous manner as many wardens were draft-dodgers who still wanted a uniform to wear.

Other kids came back to London with tales of the greedy people they had been billeted on. Knowing more mouths at the table meant extra rations, many people had taken evacuees in purely as meal tickets, eating better than before at their little guests' expense.

The rationing and shortages gave rise to a new character on the streets — the 'wide boy' — who would later evolve into the 'spiv'. You could spot them a mile off, all flashy suits and kipper ties, pencil moustaches and an ability to get anything for you — providing there was cash for them at the end of it.

By now the cinemas were full of uniformed Hollywood stars —
Bogart, Errol Flynn and David Niven amongst them. If they were the
'straight' heroes, we still had our gangster idols in George Raft,
Edward G. Robinson and my big favourite, John Garfield. Boys were
now impersonating Raft, a cigarette hanging from their lips as they
flicked a coin in the air. All the girls were piling their hair up like
Betty Grable, wearing tight sweaters like Ann Sheridan and along
with Alice Faye were our glamour dream girls.

London was now being blitzed constantly, and we all know which
part of town was getting the worst of things, situated as we were right
next to the docks and their warehouses. It was often terrifying, but
for we boys there was adventure to be found. The morning after an
air raid, my mates and I would scramble over the ruins, heaps of rubble that just the day before had been someone's house. We would
find all sorts of bits and things to take back to our homes.

As I played on one particular bomb site I noticed policemen
going through all the derelict houses. They were not trying to
clear the rubble to search for people, that had been done days
before. They were breaking open gas meters and pocketing the
coins inside. I realised for the first time that coppers could be
bent. Later I would come across plenty more corruption in the
Force. For instance, at one time I became a runner for Barney
Jacobs the bookmaker, just as my father had. I would collect bets
in the streets and take them up to Barney's place in the Minories.
It was illegal and the Police knew all about it. i would have to hand
over bundles of notes to a Police superintendent to stop the place
being raided. Similarly, my father would have to give five pounds
to the Police to ensure they did not pick him up for running the
bets. My experience meant that I never had any trust or respect for
the boys in blue from that day to this.

After one particular raid, which had forced the whole family to
spend the night in our air raid shelter, which Moggy grew flowers on
top of, we emerged from our crammed and frightened existence
like thousands of others. Our house was not there any more, just a
heap of flattened walls. Years of memories, good and bad, were just
a pile of bricks.

We were fortunate to be re-housed in nearby Sutton Road, but i
will never forget what had happened one night a short while before
we were bombed out as the family all lay asleep at our home in Fyfe
Road. We were brutally aroused by a loud banging on the back door.
Moggy got up, 'Someone's trying to break in.'

He and I, along with some of my other brothers, went outside
and looked in all directions for the intruder. He could not get away,
our place was in the middle of a terrace, and at the back ran a nine-

foot wall with barbed wire on top; behind that was Beckton Road School. When we all met up outside there was no-one there, but the banging was still going on....

There were massive dents in the back door, but no-one or nothing to be seen. A cold shiver went through us all. It was generally agreed that this was a warning — a premonition that the building was going to get bombed. How right we were. No-one has ever been able to explain that banging to me yet.

I had finally decided that I was not going to go to college any more. By this time boys of only 14, younger than me, were being directed into various work to keep the war effort going. Every tenth lad was destined to go down the coal mines — to be a 'Bevan boy'. My elder brothers had entered the services. When they came home on leave they took me out drinking. I wanted to be like them, boozing and picking-up girls. Also I had a new crowd of friends, boys who were to remain friends up to the present.

My college principal got me my first job through the Labour Exchange. Yes, testing those blasted jerrycans destined for the Army in Egypt. Baldwin's factory in Poplar paid me a princely 14/6 (72p) a week. I hated it and so did my mates who worked there. Some days we would not turn up for work, so being suspended and losing three days pay. It was at this stage that my thoughts turned towards the Merchant Navy.

'If I went in the Merchant Navy I could dodge working here at Richard Thomas,' I explained to my mates.

'That's right,' one of them agreed, 'But I don't fancy going in the Merchant Navy, they're getting sunk, aren't they?'

'So what? We're getting bombed here. Well, I'm going to have a go at it.

Off I went, up to the Merchant Navy pool. Much to my surprise, they accepted me straightaway. I had not realised how quick and easy it was to get in. Within a few weeks I was boarding my first ship. By now the Allies had opened up a second front in France and Belgium. A lot of the Channel ports had been liberated by British and Canadian troops. I found myself on the run to Antwerp, one of the most dangerous trips available. Our convoys were supplying troops at the front and taking home the wounded.

Of course, when I was back on dry land I was a hero amongst my mates, strutting as though I were winning the war single-handedly. In fact I was often peeling potatoes in between being clipped round the ear by those older than me on the ship — that is to say everyone. Yes, I was a galley boy, but it beat the hell out of testing jerrycans.

My ship was a regular on the run to the Belgian coast. Antwerp was a filthy city, full of dives and dockside bars that were nothing short of brothels. I had many adventure once ashore there, most of which ended up in fights, and all of which ended up with police of some description taking me back on board ship.

As I lay in my bunk whilst we returned to Blighty after one of these forays, there was a terrific explosion. I ran out of my cabin. 'What's happened?'

'We've been hit, it's abandon ship.'

I rushed up to the main deck, struggling with my life-jacket. I scrambled over the side into a lifeboat, which was then lowered into the sea. As we rowed away we watched our ship go down.

German E-boats had come amongst the convoy, catching our Royal Navy escort unawares. Three or four ships had been sunk.

I sat in the lifeboat, looking around. The scene was like some massive firework display. Everywhere I turned, ships were ablaze, their flames reflected in the oily water. I had been torpedoed, just like Moggy.

In that moment I grew up. Moggy might have previously given me my first pint of beer and cigarette, but now I was a man for real, so great was the impact of the swift and dramatic events and their aftermath that day.

We were soon picked up by a Dutch trawler and taken to a port on the Cornish coast.

Then I was given special leave, as were all crew who had lost their ships. I used the leave to go drinking with my mates. I was the centre of the stage, telling them all about my experiences; I was also the main attraction with the girls.

I became used to the life back on shore. I was enjoying myself, and, when the leave was over I found I did not want to go back to life on the ocean wave. Bombs or no bombs, life was to interesting on dry land. Why, had they not even started up hop picking again?

Vera Lynn might have been the Forces Sweetheart, but her tearful songs were now out of vogue, too much like heartbreak to listen to. Even the 'swooner-crooner' from across the Atlantic — Frank Sinatra — was being eclipsed by the jitterbug. And with the jitterbug dance-craze had come several armies of American troops and airmen. Compared with our own servicemen they were much more glamorous as far as the ladies were concerned; with their smart tailored uniforms, as opposed to British battledress, their huge rations and pay packets, their endless supply of nylons, Hershey bars and chewing gum, it could not be otherwise. We were resentful, quite naturally, but again, it could not be denied that their presence livened things up. We were going to win this war, and the quicker it was over with, the better. In the meantime, nobody was going to miss an opportunity to enjoy life.

People had been hardened to the violence and destruction they had seen first hand, or on the newsreels. Even later on when the atomic bombs finally ended the war, people were unshockable, after all, they had already seen Belsen, Auschwitz and Buchenwald.

During the worst days of the war for Britain, one of the most popular songs was 'It's a lovely day tomorrow'. Well people had got fed-up of waiting for tomorrow to arrive, I had, for sure. I was determined to have a lovely day each day. However, after considerable pressure from the Pool Superintendent, and with a great deal of reluctance, I eventually signed on for a ship bound for the Gold Coast.

It was on board this ship that I fell foul of the ship's bosun, a vicious, brutal bastard. We were in dock preparing for our voyage. He made my time there hell. He once caught me a blow across the face that sent me flying across the deck. There was no chance of taking him on in a fight because he was three or four stone heavier and fifteen years older than myself.

But I still thought, 'I'll have that bastard, one way or another.'

It was well known amongst the crew that the bosun always carried two sets of false teeth with him. He would never sail without them. He was terrified of going on a trip and one of his plates getting broken or lost. He knew he would not be able to get a replacement until he reached Britain again, hence the extra set. Every night he put both sets in a mug of cleaning fluid which he put on a table beside his bunk not putting them in until the next morning.

I had already made up my mind that i was going to jump ship, I was not enduring his bullying from the South coast to the Gold Coast. When we had finally been fully loaded with our cargo I knew that we would be sailing within a couple of days. I packed all my belongings into a kitbag, then made my way to the bosun's cabin. The coast was clear. I saw the mug, complete with dentures, two sets, bastard bosun for the use of, grabbed it, opened a porthole and threw the contents over the side. As I made my way down the gangplank I looked back, grinned to myself and set off to catch a train back to London.

All the journey back I could not help but smile, even chuckle out loud, about what would happen when the bosun came in to look for his teeth. It was far too late to get replacements made, he would have to sail without them.

It was not long before the train drew into London. As I looked out of the window at the bomb sites, the devastation, I felt curiously warm and comfortable inside. I had returned to my beloved city, however battered.

An air raid was in progress at the time, but this did not deter me one bit. I had no money, but I was young and fit, so I started to make my way back eastwards on foot. I could not help but notice, though I did not really know why, just how little destruction there was in the City of London compared to the almost total annihilation of the areas I was now passing through as I made my way deeper into the East End.

By now I had reached Aldgate. Realising that I was very near to the Merchant Navy's headquarters in Cable Street, a notoriously rough area at that time, I decided to make my actions known. I went into the shipping room and quite straightforwardly explained that I had jumped ship. I was summoned to the office of the Pool Superintendent. Once inside he asked me what game I thought I was playing. I bluntly replied that there was no way I was going to sail with my ship, they could do what they liked about it. The Superintendent warned me that I could be prosecuted, but I knew that was a hollow threat. I knew for a fact that they could not possibly prosecute me or send me to prison — I was under age, not eighteen yet. The Superintendent warned me again, 'You wait till you're seventeen. You're going to get quite a shock my boy.'

What he really meant was, although I did not realise it then, that far from being charged with absenteeism, or breaking any Merchant Navy regulations, I would be called up by the Army as soon as I reached seventeen and a half. But I was not interested in what he had to say, I just wanted to get home. So I asked if I could have a loan. I was answered in the negative, so I shrugged my shoulders and walked out.

Soon I was settled down at home in Sutton Road. I had a go at working for an asbestos company. Most of the lads went there because the pay was good: it worked out between £1 and £1-10-0, good money by the standards of any alternative. Little did we know that the asbestos would prove to be a long- term killer. As the years went by, many who had worked with me ended up succumbing to asbestosis or cancer. Not that the factory owners gave a damn what their products did to the workforce. They just paid a few extra bob to attract labour, knowing youngsters would beat a path to their door.

I only spent a short while working there before I found that I could make a lot more money by pulling ceilings down in bomb shattered homes round Bethnal Green. The ceilings were unsafe, so had to come down. They were then replaced with what we call ceiling boards — a novelty in those days. I relished this work.

A working gang would get up into the lofts of the properties and just start kicking down with their boots, knocking the old plaster into

46

the rooms below. We would tie handkerchiefs over our faces to protect our nostrils and throats, as the dirt and dust went everywhere; we got into a shocking state.

The building firm that was re-developing large parts of the East End, including the buildings I worked on, paid £4 a week. People flocked to work for such a fortune.

I was as pleased as Punch to get a job I enjoyed and was paid big money for doing. It never occurred to me that I could use my wages to save, to me it was just a means of going out at night and the weekend to enjoy myself even more than before. So it was that I would hang out with my circle of workmates — frequently getting as drunk as lords.

We would go down to the 'Old Queens' pub at Poplar, always making sure that we had drunk a couple of pints before we went into the bar. Inside the pub a comedian would be on, telling old jokes. We took great delight in yelling out the punch-lines just before he got to them. This would cause an uproar, which before long involved attendants coming across to where we were and throwing us out. This is what we always planned for, because we liked nothing better than a brawl with them. Once bundled outside the 'Queens', we would continue to shout and laugh before setting off to find somewhere else to drink.

Sometimes we would walk across the old Canning Town Bridge. One of our great joys was to pick up the paraffin lights that had been set down on it to warn of obstruction, and hurl them into the night air. We would follow their progress until they splashed into the Thames. Off we would wander, laughing our heads off. This was a good night out.

This was the pattern of my life for quite a while. The was was still going on, 'doodlebugs' now rained down on us, the deathly silence as their engines cut out warning that they were about to come crashing down. We lads did not care though. To us it seemed that there had always been a war on, and some days it seemed that it might go on indefinitely.

Nothing lasts forever, neither wars or wining and wenching. One day I came home from work and there was a letter waiting for me.

'You've got an official letter,' Mum informed me. It was rare enough to receive any letters at all, let alone ones with the official crown on them. The contents told me that I had to report to Romford Road Army centre for a medical. I was now seventeen and a half....

'Oh no, this is a mistake, I'm in the Merchant Navy, I haven't been away to sea for a year or so, but I'm still in.'

The next day I went up to Cable Street an asked to see the Pool Superintendent. I was shown into his office. When I told him about the Army letter he looked at me and smiled. He had not forgotten me. 'You're just one of the many. We told you what would happen when you reached this age. Now see if you can mess them about like you've messed us about.'

Chapter Four
A SQUARE PEG...

The prospect of going into the Army did not really bother me. It would be a new adventure.

I turned up at the appointed place and time for my medical. I was not worried in the least, being fit and strong, and with no intentions of trying to dodge the call-up. I sailed through the medical and was told that I would be contacted in due course.

I went home and practically forgot all about it, giving no thought to hearing from the Army again or not. Life went on as usual, going to work and then going out drinking with my mates.

Forest Gate roller-skating rink had become a favourite meeting place for young people during the war, and now we often converged there. Then a second official envelope arrived for me. Inside were travel warrants and instructions to report to Stranraer Reception Centre. Why on earth were these clots sending me all the way to Scotland?

I caught the northbound train and arrived at Stranraer Station. It was pouring with rain, it was stark, and it was miserable. There were large notices up telling all Army recruits to report to vehicles stationed outside. I made my way up the platform and out through the ticket barrier. There was a sergeant ticking names off a list as men climbed into a lorry. I joined them.

Soon we found ourselves at a camp consisting of some iron Nissen huts. Each of us was allotted a bed. After a welcome supper we were glad to turn in. I slept like the proverbial log.

The camp was roused at seven the next morning, which did not please me much. Then we were told why we had been sent to Stranraer.

Apparently we had all excelled at the short written exam given at the medical. I had forgotten all about the test. We were to be shipped to a centre in Northern Ireland to see if we had leadership potential.

After that briefing we were put through the Army treadmill; inoculation, haircuts and uniforms were given to all. Three days later we were on a ferry bound for Ulster; the Princess Barracks, Hollywood, County Down, to be exact.

It was not too long before I realised that most of the others on the course were from middle-class backgrounds, and were obviously being sent there to be trained as officers or N.C.O.s. It was also very obvious that Joe Morgan was not going to fit in.

The living accommodation in the barracks was quite rough and ready, but to me this was no worse than the conditions I lived in back home. In truth it was somewhat better than home. For most of the other recruits who had come from 'nice' homes, it was very hard to adjust.

I soon found myself in a lot of trouble about my bad language. The other recruits had not been used to hearing much in the way of swearing, so my remarks to those who wore pyjamas in bed did not go down very well. I had no pyjamas, let alone seen anyone else wear them, unless you counted actors in films.

I found that there were some other blokes from my own sort of background. It was evident they had the qualities of leadership that were being looked for, in spite of their working-class backgrounds. We quickly banded together and became the rebels of our batch of troops. We went out drinking and brawling, along with all the other things that we should not have done if we had any pretensions of being officers or N.C.O.s — part of the middle-class.

All the physical aspects of training, such as the assault courses and the square-bashing, the general slog of Army life meant nothing to me, I sailed through without problems. In fact, I excelled at those parts, as did the other working-class lads. Yet most of them did not do so well in the classrooms, although I did. But the atmosphere at the desks was more than I could stand; it was like being back at school again. Other recruits were constantly taking the mickey out of my cockney accent, and I really resented it. I hit back in the only way I knew how, by making jokes about the others.

In our off-duty hours we rebels would go out on our own, not desiring to mix with the bulk of our middle-class training company. On the rare occasions that we did bump into our social 'betters' I invariably tried to start a barney.

And so our first weeks in Ulster went by. It did not seem such a bad life to me, excepting the type of people I was being forced to mix with.

I had never been a spiritual person, always remaining rather cynical about the prospects of an after-life. To me, when you were dead, that was it. Nor did I believe in ghosts, at least, not since I was a child. Yet I had never been able to explain the dreadful banging on our back door and now, here, miles from home, I was faced with an equally odd and eerie experience.

One day we rebels were out walking, looking for a pub. We wanted to try a real old Irish pub, so that we could drink the Irish Guinness. We had been told that it was as thick as treacle, and so we were determined that we would go and get drunk on it. It seemed a normal day, and none of us had enjoyed a drink since the previous day.

50

As we trudged through the country lanes, I suddenly came over very faint. I could not understand what was happening. I stopped, and it was as though I was being told that I could go no further.

'What's the matter Joe?' one of my friends asked.

'I don't know, I've got a funny feeling.'

Then I described a little village with a barn and a boarded-up church, using quite a bit of detail, a village I was sure lay around the next bend. My friends rubbished me, but I insisted that I was right. They then geed me up until the feeling had gone before we set off again.

Around the bend in the lane was a small village. It was just as I had described it: barn and boarded-up church too.

'Must have been here before,' someone suggested.

'No, I've never been here.'

This strange occurrence and the stranger feelings have never left my thoughts.

Not long after that I got another funny feeling, but there was nothing supernatural about it. I began to realise just how unfair the system in the barracks was. Whilst the middle-class recruits were being encouraged to do well, it was apparent that the working-class intake were being virtually ignored. It dawned on me that the class structure was in some respects even more rigid and wrong than it was in civvie street. This was really my first adult taste of class distinction in such an openly prejudiced manner. It caused a smouldering resentment within me.

I reasoned as follows: 'Fair enough, if that's how they want it, I'll go my own way.' From that moment on, as far as anything to do with the Army was concerned, I did not want to know. I did the bare minimum to keep out of trouble, but always in a sullen, reluctant manner. I set out to dodge any duties I could to give me more time to enjoy myself.

I took my anger and resentment out on the others in my billet. Not a single night passed without me carrying out some trick or other. When the 'soft' recruits would walk modestly into the shower, clutching their strategically placed towel, Morgan was there to pull their modesty away, soak it, and flick its owner's more tender parts with the wet end. And of course I could not resist making a few wicked remarks about the other private's private parts.

All the tame recruits came in at night and went to bed at the proper time. On the other hand, we rebels would crawl back long after curfew, creeping in under the wire. Nearly always the worse for drink, we would then run around the barracks causing havoc. Inevitably we would be put on report, which meant being put in

51

front of our company sergeant-major and then asked to explain our conduct and attitude.

I saw this as betrayal. No matter what the others did to me, I never reported them. I would always sort the matter out for myself and expect the others to do the same. My contempt for our middle-class comrades became even stronger.

I still enjoyed the gung-ho side of our training, but I could not endure the British Army 'bull' that went with it. Of a Saturday afternoon we would cut the grass on the football pitch — with scissors. Another favourite was whitewashing the stones that marked out the sides of paths. This was degrading, especially when officers deliberately walked past kicking dust over you as you knelt painting.

One day a mate and I were whitewashing stones when we saw two officers approaching, one hitting the stones with his swagger- stick, which caused little clouds of white dust to rise up. 'Just watch, I'm going to have this bastard if he does that to me,' I promised.

'Be careful,' my mate advised. As the officers came near I raised myself up, clutching my left leg, complaining that I had cramp. As the offending officer drew level I dropped my can of whitewash, splashing his shoes and trouser bottoms.

'You clumsy oaf, you ignorant swine,' he bellowed.

'Sorry Sir, it wasn't my fault Sir, I'm in terrible pain.' The officer continued to roar and scream for a full minute before taking my name and number and then hurrying away. We collapsed in fits of laughter. The story soon became the talk of the barracks.

Soon after that my company sergeant-major called me into his office. He told me that I was a cunning little sod who was going to find himself in hot water before very long. Further, he did not know what I was doing in this type of selection barracks, but the quicker I was out, the better. And that went for the gang of ruffians that I had gathered around me. He carried on by throwing insults at me, but I did not bat an eyelid. When he had finally finished, I went away and studied the King's Regulations in detail. Soon I literally knew every trick in the book, I was a right barrack-room lawyer. The Army's authority was not going to grind me down.

All this time in Hollywood (that's a laugh, it could not have been less like its Californian namesake) seemed like an age, yet it all barely lasted three weeks. Just too many remarks about an Old Etonian who had been shy of undressing in front of the rest of the barracks, coupled with my booing a parade of Orangemen, convinced the powers that were that I did not, and would not, fit in. I was posted back to England.

Here the Army were, looking for leadership material. Whilst I was a rebel, I was also surrounded by friends who looked up to me for advice. I was a leader. The Army authorities did not have the ability to see this. I later came across a lot of ex-army officers in the guise of administrators, bureaucrats and M.P.s, most had less sense in the whole of their pompous bodies than I had in my little finger.

I was sent to Warley Barracks in Brentwood, where I finished my basic training with the rest of my regiment, First Battalion, Royal Fusiliers.

For me it was business as usual. Always in trouble, always out drinking, never bowing to discipline. Strangely enough, although the officers looked down on me in disdain, the sergeants and sergeant-majors began to like me. This was probably because I always carried out any fatigues dished out as punishment in a cheerful manner, ready for more if necessary. No-one was going to break me.

Although I was quite short in height, I was stocky with it, and I soon became known as something of a hard man.

Gradually, the Army began to leave me alone. They stopped picking me out for guard duties and stopped worrying when I failed to turn up on parade. I liked this new attitude because it meant more freedom for me of a night time and weekend.

It was the weekends especially that I and my new bunch of drinking mates would find ourselves in all manner of unlikely places, having flaked out at some stage. Even bombed air-raid shelters were not safe from our attentions when we lurched out onto the streets at closing time. Our uniforms would end up in a mess, and if we were caught it would mean more charges. This did not deter us one iota.

My basic training came to an end. The training and rough living conditions were almost luxury to an East End boy. I had always been fit so assault courses and gym were a breeze. I proved to be a natural with a gun, earning the crossed rifles of a marksman on one sleeve, with the laurel Bren gun badge on the other — this showing I was also handy with the Bren and Sten guns.

I looked forward to being posted overseas, providing it was not to go and fight the Japanese. Whether it was the atrocities I had read about, or just a young man's fear of the unknown, I do not know. I did know I was both relieved and pleased to be sent to Germany.

I was amongst the first batch of British troops to arrived in defeated Berlin. I quickly settled in, finding myself a room right at the top of a massive, old-fashioned block, the Queen Wilhemina Flats. When I entered the room it was full of cigarette smoke and already occupied by other fusiliers, who were playing cards.

'Aye aye, ain't you supposed to be on parade?' I asked.

'Who the fucking hell are you?' came back a cockney voice.

'All right, all right. I'm like you, I'm looking for somewhere I can dodge the column.'

53

'Oh well, we've got a spare bed. Where do you come from first, before we let you in here?'

'Canning Town.'

'Oh, cor blimey, I come from East Ham.'

'So where do you come from?' I asked the second card-player. 'You don't sound like a Londoner.'

'No, he's a bleedin' swede-basher,' said the Cockney, whose name turned out to be Curly Curlew.

My other new room mate was called Fred Barnes, who had done his swede-bashing in Newcastle. The pair of them took to calling me 'Smokey'.

I had a new billet and two new mates, equally adept as myself at drinking and womanising. Fred constantly worried whether his wife was being unfaithful to him. Every morning he had to be reassured that his wife was remaining faithful to him back in England, but every night he picked up a girl who, like as not, he would end up sleeping with. Next morning he would be full of guilt, still asking if his wife was behaving in the manner he expected of her but not himself.

Berlin was a terrible place. Nine-tenths of it was rubble, corpses lined the streets as people starved. It made me angry to see ordinary folk suffering so much although I could not be angry with the Germans themselves, just the bunch of idiots at the top who had taken only a dozen years to ruin that country and wrought so much destruction and death at home and abroad.

My finer feelings did not stand in the way of my street-sense, which quickly told me there was a killing to be made on the black market. Booze was easily obtainable. British soldiers were doled out hundreds of cigarettes with their pay and rations each week, just ten of which could buy a bottle of schnapps. The Red Army troops and the Berliners were equally desperate to trade. We soon discovered there was a huge black market operating right in the city centre.

One night I turned to Curly Curlew in the next bed. 'Do you know, these Russians, they're bleedin' nut-cases. Give 'em a Mickey Mouse watch and they'll give you a gold bracelet for it. Or English cigarettes they go mad for.'

'I know that, but you've got to be careful, they're gun happy. If they think they're getting caught, they'll put some bullets in you.'

'Well, we'll make sure we don't get caught. Anyway, I've got a smashing idea.'

'What's that then Smokey?'

'Well look, when do you go down the NAAFI, the dog-ends in the ashtrays, they're all good and firm, right? Now, how do you get our cigarette ration?'

'Well, in packets.'

'Yeah, come on, what else?'

'And we get some tins of cigarettes.' Curly gave a broad grin.

'You crafty bastard, I get it.'

'We cut the dog-end part off and we stuff the tin with cotton wool.'

'And then we put all the dog-ends in the tin....'

'And we put the lid on,' said Fred, who was awake, and had finally caught on.

'And off we go. A tin of cigarettes. They won't take one out because they're new tins, and we're not gonna let them handle them. The Russians'll put the tins away as soon as we hand them over.'

Retrieving dog-ends became our top priority. The other squaddies used to watch us emptying all the ashtrays. They never guessed what we were up to. After about three nights of collecting, we had bags and bags of dog-ends. Then we went around asking for empty cigarette tins, claiming we just wanted them to put bits and pieces in.

We were aided in this by the other member of our gang, a London-Irish lad called Dennis O'Keith. He did not room with us, but he was on our Bren gun carrier crew (I had also wangled Curly and Fred onto the team), and we had taken to him; he was the baby of our group. He looked like Donald O'Connor and could sing all the Frank Sinatra songs. Curly and I used to love listening to him.

When we went out on the town it was my job to see that he did not go with any prostitutes, and catch a dose, whilst Curly made sure he did not get drunk. It was a bit like the blind leading the blind, but it seemed to work.

None of us ever went on parade, did guard duties or appeared anywhere near work. It was as if everyone had forgotten we existed. Every Friday we would collect our pay and cigarettes, no questions asked.

In those early days after the War, the cigarette was king. It rapidly became the major currency, German people being only too glad to do the work they were ordered to carry out by the British Army in return for a few vital sticks of tobacco, with which they could buy food and drink. In the winter of '45/6 many Berliners starved to death in the streets. Army lorries would go round as Germans loaded the corpses of their own people onto the backs.

Tales abounded about Nazi and Red soldiers alike raping and pillaging during the closing days of the War, but I saw enough to convince me British troops were not much better. The Tommie adopted more subtle tactics than his continental counterparts, but the result was the same: if he found a starving woman, perhaps with a dying baby, he gave her a cigarette in return for intercourse. So what was that if not rape?

By night the city was transformed. Night clubs would open up where a soldier could get gloriously drunk for the cost of a packet of cigarettes. We were having the life of Riley. No buses or trams for us, we went everywhere by taxi. We smoked big cigars too. We lived like the Yankee G.I.s, because if you were prepared to forget your scruples you could make as much as they did.

I had heard about the guard duty in the Tier Garten. The idea was to stop refugees coming into the British Sector of Berlin from either the Russian Sector or the Red-occupied Eastern Germany. If the Russians caught any refugees they shot them. I realised that there was room here to earn a few bob.

We had been doing pretty well out of the cigarette racket, but it was time to move on.

'Don't forget,' I warned the others, 'We've gotta be careful. They'll (the Military Police) be looking for us. We'll 'ave to go to different parts of Berlin now. We can only do it half a dozen time, then we'll have stop. Those Russian bastards will fill us full of lead one of these dark nights.'

Some days later, we were sitting in our room. It was afternoon, and we sat around drinking beer. I started to talk about the Tier Garten duty, and how troops on it were supposed to turn refugees back, how Red Army deserters caught by our Military Police were handed straight back to the Russians, knowing they would be taken out into the woods and shot. To my mind, the M.P.s were as bad as the Nazis had been.

'You know, those refugees would do anything to get over the border.'

'That;s right,' shrewd Curly agreed, ' "Got any jewellery, a watch?" Only too glad to give it to you to let 'em go over.'

'And who gives a damn if they come over here?' I laughed.

Curly posed the problem of how to get on the guard; I had the solution.

'Leave it to me, we'll all go out on parade tomorrow morn....'

'On parade?' Fred exploded. 'We havna' been out on parade for God knows how long.'

'That's alright, we'll say we've been on education courses, alright? Those Education sergeants, they're as dumb as arseholes. You know what they are, don't you? They're all bleedin' queers, iron hoofs. They won't shop us. They don't even know who is there, and most of the soldiers just go there to have a kip anyway. So, that's what we'll do, okay?'

Next morning, out we went. The rest of the company looked at us in amazement. Even the sergeant looked. 'What are you doing here Fusilier Morgan, Fusilier Curlew, Fusilier Barnes? What the hell are you doing here, and where have you been all this time?'

'On an education course,' Fusilier Morgan replied.

'I'm sure you need an education Morgan, you of all people, the shrewdest little bastard round here. You don't need no educating.'

'Well you can ask the Education Sergeant,' I persisted.

'I heard you only went to one or two classes, and even there you caused trouble.'

'Not me Sergeant, I didn't cause no trouble.'

'Yes you did, you gave a talk on a revolution and how Royalty should be done away with. In fact you're in dead trouble my boy, because it's been reported to the company commander, and he's been asking questions about it. You could find yourself on a bleedin' charge. A right old whizzer.' I said nothing.

What the sergeant said was true. A colonel had been visiting our education class, and I had been asked to give a talk on general subjects. A few feathers were ruffled when I chose to talk about the merits of communism versus capitalism and republicanism versus Royalty. The sergeant was also right about a charge: I received 14 days confined to barracks and a severe reprimand. The whole point of the education classes were to allow soldiers to learn new ideas and be able to speak their minds on them. All that was ahead of me though, as the sergeant told us to get fell in.

Then he started giving out the guard duties. Before he got to the guard for the Tier Garten I interrupted: 'Sergeant, my Bren gun carrier has had its track thrown, and I need to get it put on. After this parade, I wonder if the crew can help me?' I figured that I knew what his reply would be.

'Certainly you can,' he smiled, wickedly, 'And when you're finished you can pack your bags, you're on a seven day tour of the Tier Garten.' He roared with laughter. I had been right.

'Cor Sergeant, be fair.'

'I'll give you "be fair". You're on the Tier Garten guard. And your own bleedin' little gang with you as well.'

We left the parade ground with big grins all over our faces.

'How the bleedin' hell d'ya do it Smokey?' Fred asked.

'Got it up 'ere,' I explained, pointing to my head. 'That's where you need it mate.'

The following day we packed our bags and set off. When we got there, the Tier Garten was filthy dirty. We were billeted in a guard room that some Red Army troops had slept in previously. It smelt as though they had not washed since the day Hitler invaded Russia. They had fleas bigger than the horses that they used to draw their waggons. Most of the ones we came across were

57

Mongolians. 'Ugly looking bastards,' I remarked to the others, 'Hope they don't get too near us.'

As expected, when darkness fell, silent figures could be seen everywhere, trying to get through the Tier Garten. When we challenged them they pleaded with us, begging not to be sent back. Just as we had predicted, they gave us their watches and rings. We let them through. At the end of our seven days we had a nice little haul to sell on the black market.

We sold our Tier Garten goodies for British Armed Forces money (B.A.F.), which we then used to buy postal orders, these being sent back to our parents for safe keeping until we went home on leave. So it was a good racket all round. The refugees were happy, we were happy. We were not alone in our enterprise either, thousands of other British, Soviet, and, I'm sure, American and French troops were doing something similar all over occupied Europe.

When we returned to our unit, we had more than just watches and rings on us. The filthy blankets we had been forced to sleep in meant we were covered in fleas, bug bites, scabies and crabs. All of us ended up in the de-lousing unit. 'We're laughing on this,' I assured the others as we examined our unwanted guests. 'We'll make sure we get on those guards as often as we can.'

The scheme seemed too good to be true, and so it proved. The Special Investigations Branch from the Military Police got wise to the vast number of postal orders going back to Britain. They raided some of their main suspects; a captain, a few N.C.O.s and half a dozen men were picked up. A court martial followed, with the captain being cashiered and most of the others earning jail sentences. One day afterwards I read in the Army newspaper that there had been a massive ring of racketeers operating throughout Germany. Thousands of pounds had been involved. 'Shrewd boys,' I thought, 'Makes us look like Sunday School kids, don't it?' Except they made one mistake that we avoided; they got caught.

The following day was a Sunday, I went with my mates up to the NAAFI in the centre of the city. There we decided to go on the razzle, so we went to a bus stop, figuring we had better tighten our belts slightly now our main source of outside income had dried up. While we stood there I saw a very pretty girl coming along the street. 'Ain't she a cracker? Look at her, she's like a film star.' As she came towards us, carrying her bag of shopping, I started to speak to her, using the usual mixture of broken German and some old chat-up line.

I did not know it, but I had just started a relationship with my future wife.

Chapter Five
EINER DEUTSCHER MAIDEN

'Guten Tag Fraulein, come on ze with me?' was my hopeful opening gambit. She said something I could not understand in return, looking at me with disdain.

'She gave you a mouthful there Smokey,' the others laughed.

'Nah, rubbish. I bet I can have it away with her.

'Bet you can't,' they said. Then, 'Well, we're not waiting around, we're going up to have a drink,' Fred and Curly decided.

Dennis had seen a blonde girl he had taken a fancy to and he and I started following the two girls along the street. We walked behind them chatting them up and gradually the girls began to smile and talk to us, slowing their steps until we were all walking together.

'What's your name? I asked my choice. 'Namen? Namen?'

'Ah, Crystal,' she replied. Then she asked me for my name.

'My name? Um, er, Ted,' I lied. I very rarely gave a girl my real name. I did not want one of them turning up at the barracks afterwards and saying 'A man named Joe has given me a baby.'

I asked her to come for a drink, but she refused. By using a mixture of German and English we managed to make ourselves understood to each other. She said she had to go home. 'I'll come home with you, we'll have some coffee.'

We carried on walking until we came to the Kant Strasse. I was determined to go to this girl's home. Yet there was something about her that made me feel uneasy. She did not seem the same as the other German girls I had been going out with, the sort that hung around the bars. She was obviously just an ordinary German woman.

Dennis in the meantime was more than laughing. He was walking arm in arm with the blonde girl, whose name was Lydia. Finally, we reached Crystal's house. I did not like the name Crystal so I kept on calling her Chris. She would keep repeating 'Chris, Chris, Crystal.' But I insisted on calling her Chris. We went into the house, the normal German type with plenty of stairs and large rooms. We spent the next few hours talking. Then Dennis and Lydia disappeared to go to her flat across the road.

'Right,' I thought, 'this is it.' Much to my surprise I got no encouraging response from Chris, she kept pushing me away, saying 'No, no, no.'

'Sod this,' I decided, looking at my watch. I was getting quite annoyed, thinking that I could be at the pub by now. but something still held me there.

Then Chris said 'I think you should go now. It is time for you to go. Will I see you again?'

'Oh yeah,' I lied again. I had no intention of going back.

I looked in a couple of dives to see if I could find my mates, but I did not see them. By half past eleven I was back in barracks. 'Blimey,' I mused, 'this is the earliest I've been to bed since I've been in Germany.' When my mates came in at two in the morning they said, 'Cor, look, Smokey's asleep already.'

'I'm not asleep. Struck out, didn't I? Should have gone with you.'

'We had a fantastic time, met some lovely birds.'

'Yeah, I knew that would happen.'

'You seeing her again?' Curly ventured.

'You must be joking.'

The following night I started to think about Chris. 'I don't know, I must be bleedin' mad.' I went to my locker and removed some tins of corned beef and a couple of bars of chocolate. Then I set out for her house. She was waiting for me.

'I'm glad you came,' she managed in her broken English. I gave her the food and went in. There, looking up at me was a little boy about a year old, with blond curly hair. 'Hello, watch this,' I warned myself. This was Chris's baby. She told me how her husband had been a right bastard to her; they had only been married six weeks when he went off with another woman, leaving his pregnant wife behind.

I stayed and enjoyed her company. But again I returned to barracks early.

We went on meeting for a week or two, and I started to miss her when we were apart. One night when I went to visit, her parents were there, Herr and Frau Dreher. They asked me all sorts of questions, but the language difficulty meant neither side was really sure what was being said. The next night I took Chris out for a drink at the NAAFI. As we walked in all the other soldiers turned to stare at Chris's beauty. I felt so proud that she was my girl. We went to the British Army pictures afterwards to see a Deanna Durbin film. I have never forgotten that night. There we were, in the middle of a country that had been ravaged by war, a country that in turn had ravaged other nations and been responsible for the death of millions, but we were sitting there like any other courting couple. That night Chris made it clear to me that I did not have to leave her house and return to the barracks. And so our love affair began.

I stopped going to the bars and seeing other women. I stayed with Chris over the next three months. We were ideally happy together. Then I had to tell her that the entire regiment was being moved. She cried and cried. 'Don't worry,' I reassured her, 'I'll put in for my leaves in Berlin rather than England, and I'll come and stay with you.'

Both battalions of the Royal Fusiliers were posted to Recklinghaesan. Within a few weeks I managed to get myself into the biggest trouble I had ever experienced in the Army. It started out as a run of the mill argument with another soldier on a train, but it carried on to the parade ground where I used violence to settle the matter. I immediately regretted it, but that did not save me from a Field-General Court Martial, especially after I refused to obey the Company Commander's orders whilst out on a route march. I knew that I had gone too far this time.

I wrote to Chris explaining that I was under arrest, so I could not visit her. I then settled down and waited for my case to be heard.

While I was waiting I began to read political books. I became more and more fascinated by the political history of the working class.

At the Court Martial I soon saw that the officers conducting it showed little if any interest in the proceedings. There was a cricket match going on outside the courtroom window, and the presiding judge actually clapped a very good piece of fielding. Yet he was supposed to be listening to the evidence in a case that would decide what would happen to me. I was not surprised at the attitude. I knew that it was nothing to do with right or wrong. It was just a case of the officer class versus the common soldier, the working class man.

What had surprised me was the severity of my sentence: two years hard labour, to be served in the infamous Beilafeld prison. The long delay I had endured whilst waiting for the trial had taken up nearly a year of my life. Fortunately this was taken into account, so my actual time to serve at Beilafeld was approximately a year. That was normally long enough to teach most squaddies several lessons.

I was escorted to Beilafeld to begin the worst period of my life.

Everything in the prison was done at the double, no inmate ever walked anywhere, he ran. This made it so easy for the guards to stick their boots out and send you sprawling to the deck. So easy that they did it constantly. And once you were on the floor, you were just that much nearer to their toecaps, so they did not miss a golden opportunity to try some unusual prisoner rehabilitation methods on your ribs.

Each day the routine of a prisoner would continue, hindered by the guards. They would wait until you had slopped out before kicking your bucket over, sending urine and excreta all over your clothes and the floor of your cell. Then you would have to clean the mess up. At meal times we were served little more than pigswill. Breakfast consisted of a foul porridge, of which the remains had a few raisins thrown in before being served up at lunchtime. The guards tried to make up for the deficiency of the food by spitting in it as you ate.

It was cruel, it was brutal, and no-one seemed to worry about it. No-one in authority ever came round to check on conditions.

Every morning we were lined up in full marching order, with all our kit. We were then hit in the kidneys with truncheons by our sadistic jailers. One of them in particular stays in the mind's eye — he was known as Anzio Pete, he made my old Merchant Navy Bosun seem a charmer by comparison. He was the biggest sadist I have ever met. He had a yellow streak down the middle of his back, but then all the guards did. The type of people who do those jobs are generally cowards. Before they went on leave they used to remove their Prison Guard shoulder flashes because one of them had been dumped overboard by some squaddies on a ship going home.

I lived in a dormitory cell with six other prisoners, who shared a bucket with me as well. We never knew if the guards would burst in during the night and throw the contents of our sophisticated latrine over the beds or not. This style of treatment went on day in and day out. My weight began to drop dramatically.

I managed to get a letter out to my father telling him about the officer who had clapped the cricket match during the trial. Moggy was shrewd enough to send the letter on to a Major Fred Readman, who wrote a column for the Sunday Pictorial. Major Readman took the matter up with the War Office.

One day I was invited into the Commandant's office.

'You've been writing letters to the newspapers,' he informed me.

'No,' I replied.

'Are you sure?'

'Yes.'

'Well you'll be hearing from me. Now get out.' Out I doubled.

Most of the time that I remained banged up I spent reading. More and more I developed my skills as a barrack-room lawyer. I knew the rules better than the guards, I would quote rules to them as my only means of defence. They hated me for it.

I used my leadership abilities to organise a party of prisoners to go to church service on Sundays. The prison chaplain was ever so pleased to see his message was getting through, with his small church packed out. What he did not appreciate was that we would have watched paint dry if it meant getting out of our cells for a while.

We would really enjoy the hymn singing, especially 'On a Hill Far Away'. We would infuriate the guards by adjusting the chorus to 'fucking great hill, fucking great hill.' We then roared out with laughter, despite the fury of the guard who would run up and down the aisle, telling us to shut up and banging his 'betsy' as the rubber truncheons were called. The embarrassed chaplain would try to calm the guards down. Scenes like this gave me great delight, one of the few ways I had of retaining my spirit and getting my own back.

I had served about three months of my sentence when I was again brought before the Commandant. He told me that I was being discharged and that I should report straight back to my battalion. I later found out that the Sunday Pictorial had forced the War Office to re-open my case. On re-examination of the facts, the sentence was reduced to three months. I had served my time, I was free of Beilafeld.

Back at the battalion, rather to my amazement, I found that I had become something of a hero amongst the old sweats, although the new squaddies fresh from home had been advised to keep away from me, as I was a villain just out of prison.

On the second day of my liberty I went in front of the company commander. I was treated with a good deal more respect than previously. He told me that the Army had no intention of trying to make a soldier out of me. I should bide my time and wait for my demob.

This suited me down to the ground. I spent my remaining days keeping fit by playing football, something I was very good at. I turned out for both the battalion and regimental sides, giving the Army something to be proud of in Joe Morgan after all. During this time I was given no guard duties, nor was I expected to attend parade or do anything else really. To all practical intents they did not with to know me — it was mutual. I spent my time away from the football pitch by drinking with my mates, who similarly were just waiting to be discharged from the duties of the King's shilling.

I was due a fortnight's leave, so I asked if I could spend the first half of it in Berlin. Much to my surprise this was agreed, and very soon I found myself on a train steaming through the Russian zone to Berlin.

I had kept in touch with Chris throughout my incarceration by means of the few letters that I was allowed to write, but I had not told her that I was on my way to Berlin. I arrived at her flat, not knowing whether she would be there, but she was. Seeing me at the door, she could not believe her eyes. Screaming with joy she flew into my arms. The first thing she noticed after our time apart was my weight loss. She began straightway by feeding me up. There was not much food to be had, just ersatz bread with a few bits and pieces. But what Chris had she gave to me. I was hungry after the train journey and ate it gratefully.

We then spent seven days of bliss together, easily the happiest in my life. At the end I promised her that I would not go out with any other girls, and also that when I returned from my leave in Canning

Town I would spend as much time as possible with her. I asked Chris if she would come to where I was stationed. I knew this would mean her crossing the Russian lines, and I knew how difficult that would be. I would not be able to get a pass for her, she would have to sort that out herself, if she was determined to come. I did not know at this stage what a fighter Chris would turn out to be. I suppose I should have guessed when she told me what happened when Berlin lay shattered, waiting for the conquerors of the Nazis to appear.

Chris and her family had waited with absolute terror for the Russians to enter Berlin. Like all Berliners they prayed that the British and American armies would arrive first. They had heard stories of Russians looting and murdering and raping women and children. Even the terrible bombing and shelling that had turned the city into a mass of rubble was not as frightening as the fear of the Mongol Hordes in the Red Army that were now on the outskirts of Berlin.

When their conquerors did turn up, Chris and her family were herded into the street — men on one side and women and children on the other. One Mongolian soldier pointed to Chris, Harry and some other babies, and started to give them biscuits. A woman whispered to Chris, warning her not to take any as they were obviously poisoned. The soldier chewed one biscuit to show they were okay before offering others to the children. Other troopers were not so friendly.

The Mongolians often walked about with their private parts hanging out, raping any woman they fancied was and when they pleased. Chris saw one woman being raped by a group of soldiers, and when the husband tried to stop them a rifle butt was crashed into his head. They then took turns to rape the woman before returning to the man and crushing his skull completely. Chris grimed her face with coal dust and wore a shawl over her head to avoid such unwarranted attentions; fortunately this worked. Her sister was not so lucky, as a devout church goer she merely prayed for deliverance, but this was to no avail when she too became a rape victim of the soldiers.

The family did not dare move out of the home by night for fear of attack. Screams for mercy could often be heard outside. Some women tried to tell the soldiers that they had V.D., in a vain hope of escape, but to their amazement and disgust the soldiers would pour vodka over their private parts as a crude disinfectant and then carry out their assault anyway.

Gunfire was another common sound, even though the Nazi army had been defeated. The Russians had been given the green light by their senior officers to treat Berlin as an open city where they could do virtually as they pleased. Killing and looting were the order of the day. Law and order was nil, and the will to live was very nearly destroyed.

Normality did not return until the British and Americans arrived, with the city being divided into sectors, each under the control of one of the Allied armies. People began a mass exodus from the Russian sector towards those of Britain, America and France.

Chris and her family were in the British sector from the beginning. It was not long before patrols were started to stop movement between the sectors. The western Allies began to clear up the mess that the Russians had not bothered with, removing the corpses of Russians and Germans that had been left to rot in the streets.

Chris has always hated and feared the Russians ever since, yet whenever a T.V. programme comes on depicting the Russian way of life Chris watches enthralled, becoming emotional when she sees the suffering that they have gone through as a people. Even more pitiful is when she sees film of the last days of the war and just after. Nearly 50 years on she still shudders and cries at the memories.

When I got back home I learned from my father how he had enlisted help to obtain my release. The whole episode just reinforced his hatred for the bureaucrats who were running the country, running the system. Moggy was deeply involved in the local Labour Party by this time. He would tell me that the only way we could bring about change in Britain was by getting actively involved in the working-class political movement in order to destroy the old system from within. I was interested in what he had to say, but more immediate personal matters pressed on my mind. My main concern was to get back to Western Germany and see Chris.

I told my folks about Chris and my love for her. They did not like the idea that much, especially Mum, but they were aware that there was little they could do about it. Perhaps they hoped that once I had left the Army I would forget all about her.

When I returned to Recklingshaesan there was a letter from Chris waiting for me. In it she said she was going to make her way through the Russian lines and try and join me at the beautiful village of Isalohn, not far from my unit.

Shortly afterwards I was out with my mates when a soldier came over to me. 'Do you know a girl called Crystal?' he asked.

'Yeah,' I said, expecting that he was going to say he had met her in Berlin.

'Well she's waiting outside.'

I could hardly believe my ears. I went outside and there she was, with a bag that was almost as big as she was. She looked so pitiful. I took her in my arms and comforted her, then led her away to a bar where I bought her a whisky.

I found Chris somewhere to spend the night and stayed with her. She told me all about how she and her companions had made their way across the frontier, and how terrified they had been when captured by the Russians. I listened enraptured and appalled to think what she had gone through to get to me. We cuddled up.

We had discussed how Chris would get to West Germany, but could not find an easy answer. Her mother had said she would care for Harry while Chris went away, which would not be too long, as Joe was due to get demobbed in the foreseeable future.

Then from a friend Chris found out that if you paid money a guide would take you through the Russian lines. Chris paid the money. She set off with a group of about a dozen men, women and children, aware that people had been shot by the Russians doing the same thing and less.

They went through a dark forest, often crawling in snow and slush, warned to keep quiet, even if in pain, as the patrols were constantly on the lookout for groups such as theirs. They travelled through the night, then the guide said to them they were on their own. Told that as long as they kept off the path they would not be spotted, the party would soon reach West Germany. However, they quickly floundered in a snowdrift, women and children screamed, the helpless fugitives were quickly surrounded by the inevitable Russian patrol.

They were taken to a nearby hut and then interrogated by an officer. He wanted to know why they were trying to get to the west. He seemed quite sympathetic, but he must have seen the fear in their faces. He appeared to believe the stories about relatives in the west, and the ID papers were in order. He sternly warned them all that they would be transported by train back to Berlin, where they would be dealt with by the Russian Control. This terrified everyone, but there was nothing they could do.

Surrounded by armed guards they were taken to a railway station and left standing on the east-bound platform. The guards were posted outside the station to make sure no-one escaped. Chris and the others could hardly believe their eyes when a train pulled into the station at the opposite side, west-bound. There were no Russian guards on either platform or the bridge over the line. So they started walking towards the bridge, trembling with fear, expecting to be stopped at any moment, but they were not. Everyone wept with relief as they boarded the train and it pulled away, to freedom. Chris will never know if the Russian officer had taken pity on them, deliberately leaving the bridge over the line unguarded, or whether luck had smiled on all those desperate souls. Either way, she was safe with me now.

Next day I found Chris some permanent lodgings. I started to spend most of my time with her, as the Army's demands on me were few and far between. It was a beautiful spring, so we often spent our time just walking and talking.

Then bureaucratic inefficiency raised its bowler hatted head, though this time it acted in my favour; it seemed that my period of service in the Merchant Navy counted towards my overall National Service. This had not been taken into account when I was given my demob number. This had now been discovered, which meant that I was to be released much earlier than I expected. The day after they told me, in fact.

I rushed over to tell Chris. She started sobbing. 'I'll never see you again,' she cried. 'Yes you will,' I assured her. 'I'll send you money and you can come over to England. We'll get married.'

Still she cried, she was uncertain what to do. Then she said 'I must get back to Berlin.'

'I'll arrange for you to go on a military train; there'll be none of your crawling back this time.'

I went to my company commander and explained all about Chris, telling him that we planned to get married. Normally the authorities were naturally reluctant to believe such stories, but this time they did. Chris was given a pass so that she was able to travel back to little Harry in comfort and safety. I had come to regard the boy as my own son by now. He in return called me 'Papa', and I could not wait to see him arrive with his mother in the East End.

We said our emotional goodbyes to each other. Chris went back to Berlin, to see Harry, who she had missed so much. He was overjoyed at her return. Chris cried and hugged him, promising that they soon would be together with me for always.

I said farewell to my mates in the Fusiliers. Then it was on to the demob centre in Holland. When I arrived I was told there had been a mistake, I could not go home after all.

I was shattered. All my dreams of getting out of the Army had suddenly come to a halt. I was so near and yet so far. I walked over to where soldiers were climbing into lorries that would make the last leg of the journey to the docks, some were friends from the Fusiliers. Now they were off across the Channel, and I was stuck in the transit camp. For the first time in my service life it was all too much emotion for me to bear. As I turned and walked away the tears were beginning to well up inside.

I went to the Orderly room and asked the duty corporal whether he had heard anything. 'No, and I doubt there will be anything 'til tomorrow, he said. 'All we can do is send for a message that your papers are genuine. There was no record of you on the files so we can't let you on the boat.' I felt like screaming, but I knew it would not do me any good.

'What a poxy Army this is,' I informed the world in general.

'No good you doing your nut mate, there's nothing we can do.'

I did not even feel like going to the NAAFI for a drink. I went to my room and lay on my bed, broken in spirit. All I could think was 'God, how I hate the Army. I hate it! And I hate what it's done to me.'

I thought about the nights in prison when I had dreamt I was back in civvy street, only to wake up in the morning and realise where I was. That was the feeling I had now, the same crushing disappointment. Would I ever get out?

True, there had been some good times, but even they were what I had made for myself with my friends. I felt that the Army had done no favours for me. All it had given was pain and heartbreak. I had been in Beilafeld, guaranteed to break a man if anything could, but this cock-up was the final straw. I felt broken and beaten at last.

Yet another morning in khaki arrived. After I had eaten breakfast I made my way to the Orderly room again, far from optimistic. 'Have you heard anything yet Corporal,' I asked the current duty holder.

'What's your name?'

'Fusilier Morgan 14187618.' That number is indelibly printed on the memory.

'Yes, we've had a signal about you, it's all okay. It came through last night, about half-past six.'

I could not believe my ears. 'That rotten bastard of a corporal who was here last night said he hadn't heard anything, and wouldn't hear anything 'til the morning. So I could have been in time to get that draft that went at seven o'clock.

'No, we wouldn't have been able to get all the paperwork done in time.' The corporal was obviously covering up for his colleague.

So right up to the end they were bastards, but I controlled my rage and put on a brave face.

'Okay Corporal, when can I go?'

'You'll go with the draft tonight.'

That day seemed like a month. At last it was time for me to go, and I was on a boat bound for Hull. We docked and were sent on to a demob centre at York. There we were told that there was a train leaving at then that night, but that anyone who wanted to stay overnight could catch the morning train. Nobody volunteered to stay the night.

I was one of the first to be processed. We were given our papers and our ration books along with some money and the usual pinstriped suit. We were told to keep our greatcoats, our battledress and one pair of boots. Once on the train home we all cheered, opened the windows and threw all our Army clothes out onto the railway track. Common sense should have told us that we could at least keep them for doing work, but at that time all we wanted to do was clear the last vestiges of the Army out of our lives.

When the train pulled into London I felt so happy that I wanted to run all the way home. I felt like shouting with joy. The only good things I had got out of the Army were the friendships I had made and the fiddles we got into, and of course, most important of all, it was how I had met Chris. Now all the other elements of it seemed like a bad dream to be forgotten as soon as possible. My elation gave way to a tiredness that swept over me as I trudged wearily through the streets in the small hours of the morning. But I was free and my own man.

Quietly I let myself into the house. My father shouted out asking who it was. 'It's alright Dad, it's me.'

'What you doing home boy?'

'I've been demobbed, I sent you a letter.'

'Well we haven't got it. We'll have a chat tomorrow.'

'Okay Pop. Goodnight. Goodnight Mum.' I went off to bed and straight to sleep without a thought in my mind.

'Am I on leave? Am I really out of the Army, or is it just a dream?' were my first thoughts the following morning. In later life, many ex-soldiers and sailors I spoke to told me they shared that feeling, so damaging had been the impact of the Services on their lives.

At the demob camp they had told us that it might take us months to get acclimatized to civilian life. 'They must have been joking,' I was thinking later that day. 'It hasn't taken me five bleedin' minutes.'

When I told my parents that I intended to marry Chris, it was my mother who was not at all happy. Moggy took it very well, but Mum resented it. This was understandable because she had actually seen her own brother and sister-in-law blown to pieces in the Barking Road by a German bomb. They had all been in a pub together and were just going to walk to another pub across the road. Moggy had stayed behind for a minute on a bit of business, and Mum stayed with him. At the moment when her brother and his wife walked into the other pub it received a direct hit. Everyone in the pub was killed. This and our own bombing-out did not endear any German to my mother.

As far as I was concerned I was going to marry Chris. There was nothing to argue about, nothing to discuss. It was my life, I had made up my mind, and that was that.

'If the boy wants it, that's all there is to it,' Moggy explained to her. 'It's got nothing to do with you.' So Mum grudgingly accepted the situation. Then I told her that Chris was pregnant.

'Ah, and is this why you're marrying her?'

'No it's not. No, that wouldn't worry me.'

'No, I'm sure it wouldn't.'

I realised that if I was ever going to get Chris over to England then I had better get things moving. I went to the War Office and asked what the procedure was. They gave me some documents to sign and told me that I would have to pay the fare. All the procedures took time, and as the weeks of waiting went by I carried on with my normal life. Namely, drinking every night, one long round of drinking. I had no thought of getting a job until every last penny of my demob pay had run out. I did not even think about a wedding or saving for a rainy day.

In the meantime Chris had paid a social visit to a nephew in Berlin's eastern sector. He was a fairly high-ranking official in the ruling Communist Party. When Chris got up to return home, he suggested that she stay the night, as it was quite late. Chris nearly agreed, but then said no. That night the Russians imposed a much harsher curfew and effectively started the Berlin Blockade. If Chris had stayed with her cousin, she would have been trapped in the eastern sector.

I sent Chris a telegram, telling her to leave Berlin before the Russians starved the western half into surrender. This coincided with the start of the RAF and USAAF airlift of supplies into Berlin, and it was thanks to one of the RAF Dakota aircraft involved that Chris and Harry were able to fly out of Berlin.

Mind you, things were not quite as straightforward as that. Chris got the ticket I sent out to her and then had to wait weeks before the final boarding permission required was granted.

One day the British Civil Commission informed her she could leave the next morning. Almost the first person she saw was her father in the street, she told him her news. They went home and packed four cases, two bags and then a rucksack with Harry's needs.

All the preparations had to be made quickly, with so little warning given. This would be goodbye to a city where the electricity was being rationed by the Russians, who controlled the power station. Only four hours electricity a day — two hours in the morning and another two at night. Farewell to all Chris had known in Germany, both good and bad.

The Dreher family used a pushchair and pram to take the cases down to the despatch terminal, where Chris and Harry would be put on a coach which would take them to the aircraft waiting to fly back to its base in Hanover. At the terminal, the officer checking movement papers asked where Chris was going to. 'Canning Town,' she replied, everyone laughed. Chris wondered if she had pronounced it properly. When asked where she was from, she told the officer 'Charlottenburg'. Everyone laughed again.

All her portable possessions packed onto the coach, Chris looked out of the window to see her mother crying as she helped Herr Dreher wheel the pram and pushchair back to their home. The coach started up and set off towards the airstrip.

Once on board the Dakota, she and four year old Harry had to sit on the floor, but after all they had been through, that minor discomfort mattered not one bit.

The Dakota landed at Hanover, and Chris and Harry were taken to a transit camp, where they were unceremoniously de-loused.

Because of new British Government regulations, Chris would not be able to go to England and marry me unless she left German soil by the 31st of July, 1948. The new nationality rules demanded that women like Chris had to have left their native country for at least five months by 1st January 1949, otherwise they would not automatically be granted British Nationality, but have to apply for it. Heeding the advice I had put in a letter to her, Chris went over the border to Holland on the last day of July.

Once in Holland, she got a boat for England. Unable to speak hardly any English, yet here she was, with just her young son for companionship, as they sailed across the channel on a craft full of people who spoke in an alien babble. All she could make out was the call of a man she thought was selling matches.

She had got on a boat-train that left Germany to stop at the Hook of Holland. Somehow Harry had managed to get covered in tar, Chris had to change him into his best clothes in the middle of the train corridor as it stood at Osnabrück station.

The ticket collector took pity on them, and escorted the lonely, bewildered pair to a first-class carriage, where he sat them down opposite a suited man, who turned out to be an army officer on leave. The officer helped Chris with her cases. Chris then tried to feed the stubborn Harry with what little food she had.

The train reached its destination, Chris and Harry were the last passengers allowed on the ship. Once again, a lack of seats meant sitting on the floor.

A woman came up and told her that all the German money she had was useless, she would not be able to buy anything with it. Harry was thirsty, so Chris took him to a wash basin to drink some water. Eventually they set foot in England. Another train took them to Liverpool Street, where Chris alighted with someone she could talk to properly at last. She had met up with another German girl and her British fiance, who hailed from Brighton.

71

They were not going Chris's way, but they kindly loaded her cases into a luggage locker for safe keeping, then put her in a taxi, got in with her and told the driver to make for Canning Town.

It was a hot day, all the local children ran up to look at the taxi when it pulled up outside my house. The helpful couple told Chris not to worry about the taxi fare, then said goodbye as they drove back to catch a train for Brighton. Chris will never forget the kindness of those two strangers, who she had not seen before or since.

Nobody knew just when Chris was going to turn up, she was unable to send a telegram, and we did not have the luxury of a telephone. I was not at home at the time, but Mum was. She greeted Chris in a traditional East End way, 'Would you like a cup of tea?'

Chris had left her world for mine now, but how different her background was from mine….

Chapter Six
WELCOME TO AUSTERITY

The country I had enticed Chris to in 1948 was not only different from post-Hitler Germany, it was a world away from the Britain that had existed in the 'thirties. Chris had left behind the funeral rites of the Nazi Reich to attend the muted and protracted death of the British Empire.

None of that really bothered any of us when I walked through the front door to find my intended wife and son sitting with my old Mum. I was just so glad that my beautiful woman was here with me, home.

After all Chris's struggles, I suppose I was a sight for sore eyes. It was a lovely, sunny day outside and I was in a white, short-sleeved shirt, tanned from spending so much of my free time outdoors. So first impressions of life in tropical Canning Town must have exceeded all expectations after grey Charlottenburg.

Chris and I set up camp in the upstairs front room that Mum had cleared out for us.

Everyone in the family took to Chris immediately — with one notable exception. My brothers were captivated by her, my sisters liked her, if only for her clothes, which were far better than anything the young Harold Wilson at the Board of Trade would allow to be sold in British shops — all the decent stuff was for export. Moggy and Chris got on especially well. Even Mum, the odd one out, grudgingly turned around her initial antagonism to friendship, although it took some time.

Immigration officers took Chris's passport from her and said she would have to get married within three weeks or leave again; they did not seem to trust anyone's motives.

I had used up the last of my service money, so I had to look around for a job in the building trade. I found employment, and managed to get the afternoon of Friday, 20th of August off to attend my own wedding. I was still skint, so I had to borrow £2 from Mum for a plain gold ring. I was to work until two in the afternoon, then it was straight down to Stratford Registry Office for the ceremony. The registrar went slowly through the words of the service so that Chris could understand. I had to put my age on the marriage certificate, which was a bit of a blow, because now Chris could see that I had lied to her about my age, she was only marrying a boy called Joe, not older, sophisticated 'Ted' who she had met that day in Berlin at the bus and train terminal.

Back home Mum had provided some corned beef sandwiches for everyone, and, more importantly, plenty to drink. We had just the three wedding presents, my elder sister, Liz, gave us a milk jug and sugar bowl, and one of my brothers had brought a photo- frame. The rest could not afford anything, but promised they would buy presents as soon as they were able to. Chris sometimes reminds me that she is still waiting for them!

Still, at least she had her ring. Years later, there was a song that came out entitled, 'When your old wedding ring was new', it became Chris's favourite tune. She would look down at her hand with all the expensive rings on it that I had bought over the years, and then she would look at that plain, two-quid gold ring, worth more to her than all the rest.

We even had a few photographs taken, but could not afford to pay for them, we have nothing to show our children and their children, so all that remains are the ring and the memories of one of the happiest days of our lives.

That night the pair of us went out to a pub. On our way home we stopped at a friend's. While we were there he and his missus had a terrible row because he would not answer her at the wedding. It ended with his wife getting a clout. Chris was shocked, but as I told her, 'That's normal'. She must have wondered then and there what she was letting herself and Harry Morgan (name changed by deed poll) in for.

The times ahead would be rough, but she stuck to me and we weathered all the storms we went through. Yet in those early days, the East End way of life must have been perplexing for a girl from an entirely different background.

Christal had been born in 1922 into the Dreher family, on Christmas Eve, the youngest of three sisters and a brother. The family had already lost another little girl in infancy, so the birth of a new girl seemed doubly blessed, as if to make up for the painful loss. Chris's brother, Max, thought his dead little sister had returned, saying, 'Father Christmas has brought her back'.

Whilst she was still in swaddling, Chris's father came in one day and said to her mother 'We have a place, come'. They had to pack immediately to go and live in a new house which was owned by the iron and steel foundry where Herr Dreher worked. He had started as a crane driver there but worked his way up to telephonist.

He had fought in the First World War, often sending parcels home with his letters. Frau Dreher would read the letter inside the parcel first, leaving the other contents on a table. On one occasion, Elsa, the tomboy of the Dreher girls, took a big bread knife out of the parcel and started threatening the other children with it.

Herr Dreher survived the War and his family survived Elsa and the knife. He joined the foundry, and the hard work paid off with a new company house at Malaparna, a village full of booty that Frederick the Great had stolen from others around Europe, like the hanging bridge that crossed the river that flowed through the village and on into the Oder. The locals said it was the oldest hanging bridge in Germany.

Despite the presence of the foundry, Malaparna was virtually a rural paradise. The Dreher three-bedroomed house was on the end of a row built near the forest. Chris's father had a flagpole outside the house, where starlings used to sit and wake everyone up in the morning.

Inside there were cellars for the coal, vegetables and preserves. The coal came free once a month, left outside to shovel into the cellar, courtesy of the foundry.

With the house came a nice garden, full of asparagus, potatoes and cabbage. The garden was large enough for them to keep livestock as well: 60 chickens, 30 ducks and geese, and even three beehives. Sometimes the queen bee would fly off and take her swarm with her. This meant that someone would have to dip a goose wing in water, and then use it to push the bees into an empty bucket and cover them with cloth until father came home. Mother would never do this — she had been stung too often in the past.

Since here father was always in work, Chris's family did not want for anything, so others thought them rich. Yet her two elder sisters both had to sign-on as unemployed when they left school, work being hard to come by in slump-hit Germany. When they went to sign on they had to take sandwiches, as queues were so long.

Chris went to a protestant school, walking to class each morning by way of the foundry. She would walk right through the casting lines, her father's office in the middle like a little island. Above, huge kettles of molten metal swung by on chains pulled by the men on the ground. Chris would often stop to watch their progress across the foundry.

As Chris got older, she acquired a bicycle which she pedalled to school.

Chris can remember her father taking pictures of her and the other Dreher children in front of their flagpole. The brown matt photos showed them holding a big sign that said 'Ya!', which in this case was to show support for Hitler in the 1933 elections. Other activities the innocent Christal took part in were the distribution of the ten copies of the illustrated Nazi magazine she was given, and 'Die Sturmer', another fascist publication which contained grotesque distortions of the Jews. Hitler was sowing the seeds of his next generation of Germanic elite by indoctrination from an early age, certainly Chris was oblivious of the sinister implications of these colourful and glamorous publications.

Chris was also encouraged to join the BDM (Bundes Deutscher Maiden), a female version of the Hitler Youth, when she was quite small. Too young for a uniform, in fact. Fortunately her interest in the BDM was minimal, and she soon had more interesting things to do.

In 1935 Grandfather came to stay with the family for a year. Yet he was not very keen on the country life, being an old Berliner who preferred to be back in the public park, playing dominoes with his cronies. So when he came to say his goodbyes to this daughter's children, little Christal had no idea that she would one day follow him on the train journey to the capital.

At that stage of her development Chris was more interested in the homely concerns of going out to play and avoiding the occasional clout that came her way. This was a source of vexation to her parents, who already had one tomboy in Elsa, so they did their best to make a young lady out of their Christal.

Mother was always good at making dresses out of old material, so good that she managed to kit Chris out in something different to go to church in each week. Chris would always fidget when she was made to stand on a chair for the fitting. Her mother would clout her whilst her father would remark, 'You ungrateful child'.

Unfortunately Chris continued to fidget and wilfully run around outside in a most un-ladylike manner, encouraged as she was by the presence of the local children. Her parents were wary of them, after all, they had no shoes and spoke the 'Wouter Polish' dialect common in the district.

Chris had sandals but wanted to be like her classmates, so she often kicked her footwear off. Equally often she would come home with cut feet, running into the house screaming 'blood, blood'. That was another cloutable offence.

In 1937 Chris left the local school for the rarified surroundings of a finishing school amongst the giant hills of Riesenburger, which was far away from home, near the Czech border. She should have stayed at the finishing school from 14 through to 18 years old, but in fact she barely attended for two years. Her Dreher succumbed to the fumes he was constantly surrounded by in the foundry. He could not work in the office any more. This left the family nearly broke, Chris had to return home. This was good news as far as she was concerned, for she hated her finishing school.

It was the discipline demanded of Chris that was not to her liking. The school was run by an order of Protestant sisters on quite strict lines. When she first saw the school from the carriage that brought

76

her up from the station below, Chris might have got a clue about the nature of the place by its forbidding medieval outline.

Her sisters also attended the school, and they would have told her of how just forty girls were taught within the confines of three large castle buildings. The school was split into four 'houses' — Anenemous, Ancien, Edelweiss and Altrose, each comprised of ten girls. Her sisters would have also told her how the nuns also ran an orphanage there, and that the place had previously been a mental asylum for gentlemen, who were conveniently detained far from the genteel world of their families. All this, and much more they would have told her, but nothing could have prepared her for the routine she would have to follow against her wilful personality.

The day started early for the girls, with just a slice of bread for breakfast, although Chris made sure she always got crust on hers. Chris would take her hated uniform out of the wardrobe that had previously belonged to her sister Borgia. Lessons only took up the morning, but were conducted under the strict hand of the nuns, who hit first and asked questions later. Chris was always being hauled up in front of the mother superior for disobedience. Chris found it difficult to concentrate, so consequently she never passed any of the quarterly exams that had to be taken in each subject before the next one was begun. Her afternoons were taken up with instruction in those arts and skills deemed to make a young girl into a 'lady', sewing, cooking, table manners, forms of address and the like.

Sunday was of course a church day. All the girls would have to line up outside the church while the bell rang across the hills to announce the morning service. After everyone else had taken a pew and the bell had stopped they trooped in, aware that all eyes were on them.

Recreation came by way of walking around the local hills and enjoying the impressive views they afforded. Some days it was so clear that the sea could be made out in the hazy distance. Towering above everything else was the beautiful mountain, Schneecoppen, which as its name suggest, had a snow covered peak all year round. It was while Chris took these walks that she witnessed Czech border guards putting in wooden posts and digging ditches in the vain hope that they could keep Hitler's panzers out.

The girls were not allowed to talk to anyone else outside of the school, not even the orphans or any visitors to the orphanage. To Chris it sometimes seemed like a prison, surrounded by the thick wooden walls of the castle, having read the penknife carvings of the former inmates a thousand times.

Eventually the news of her father's illness came. It was time to go back into the real world. Even then, the vicious elements that lurked

77

above Schneecoppen conspired to prolong her misery — the horse and carriage arrived to take her through the heavy shown that had fallen, and took her safely to the station, but the trains could not cope with the weather. She had to stay in the local inn until the lines were clear.

Chris was glad to be home, but even there it could snow very heavily at times. She could remember the snow often falling so heavily for so long that when it stopped she could not see over it from the paths her father cleared from the house. School could only be reached by horse-drawn sled on those occasions.

Chris gratefully finished her schooling, but she needed a job. Her sisters had been unemployed, and Frau Dreher was determined that her youngest was not going to end up in the same boat. Chris was sent to be a nanny to some children who had been cared for by her great-cousin until her recent death. It was a job, it was local, but it was not going to carve out a great career for a restless young soul.

Yet Chris counted her blessings, she had a loving family, her father was strict but fair, her mother the typical house frau who believed in devoting all her energies to clothing and feeding her children and showering them with love, the food and warmth and love being the blessings of God. Her childhood had largely been a happy one in a moderately well-off area that had avoided the worst effects of the Great Depression and the excesses of the Nazi's rise to power. Perhaps that is why the area was fully behind Hitler.

To Chris and the other Dreher children, Nazism was just a colourful mix of flags, rousing music, parades and smart uniforms. Above all that, their father would point out to them how Hitler had solved the country's economic problems and given the Germans pride in themselves again. Rumours of the treatment of Jews and socialists were just that, only rumours. Chris had much to thank her lucky stars for, but her personal life was about to change and go off in a new direction, one that would end with her experiencing first hand the price that had to be paid for being a citizen of the Third Reich. The glories of the Nazi empire and economic cure were being bought at a price, a price her father could not warn her about, but they would all have to pay it, and the cost would be heavy.

It was 1937, Chris had not been a nanny for long when one day a friend of Frau Dreher's came in to say that she was going through Berlin, she offered to take a letter or a message to Borgia, who was living and working there. Frau Dreher's response must have surprised everyone else. 'Take Christal with you — she can get a job there.'

So it was that Chris had only about an hour to pack, not even having enough time to say goodbye to her friends. Soon she found herself getting off the train in Berlin. She went to stay with Borgia at first, who told her to get a job in a big shop that had just moved to larger premises.

The shop, Werner Mueller, took Chris on, which is what her mother had hoped would happen. Werner Mueller had retained their old premises, a shop-cum-house, and it was here that Chris and the other shop girls slept, on beds in the old downstairs department of the store. Borgia lived across the way and used to call them to get up in morning shouting out of her kitchen window. Chris would walk to the new shop, a delicatessen. She found out that her mother had worked just across the road as a young girl. Chris worked hard, now that she was not in the classroom. It was her job to scrub everything that got dirty in the shop.

Her social life was opened up by the contact with lots of other young working people. She went out with lots of the boys from other shops.

In 1938 her father got a post as a commissionaire at some flats by the government buildings near the burnt-out shell of the Reichstag, which still stood as an ironic symbol of Germany's loss of democracy. A flat in the buildings went with the post, so the Drehers were nearly all back together again.

Then came the war. Max, Chris's brother, joined the Luftwaffe. He became a test pilot. His life ended when his neck was broken by the impact of a crash on a test flight. One of his colleagues had walked away from an identical accident — he was just a bit taller than Max, so the impact hit him across the back, which absorbed the pressure — such was the fickleness of fate during those war years. Today Chris has a grandson now who is the very image of Max, he is going to train as a pilot for the Fleet Air Arm.

The war years were at first full of excitement and victories; loud music would interrupt radio programmes to herald details of land and naval victories. it seemed to some that Hitler was God. Chris's mother's feet were on the ground — she would always feel sorry for the mothers of any side's servicemen who had lost their lives. Yet the newspaper and radio propaganda constantly reinforced the feeling of rightness about what was going on.

Chris used to go out to listen to the big bands in the evenings, although Hitler had forbidden dancing during the duration of the war. One of Chris's favourite band leaders so shocked the Nazi establishment with his 'wild' music that Hitler called him 'The white Negro'. If Chris was not going out with a boy friend then she would stay in and listen to her Marlene Dietrich records. She adored Dietrich. Many years later, I took Chris for a holiday to Paris, and whilst we waited for our delayed flight to be called we saw Dietrich in the airport lobby. Chris went up to her and said in German, 'Madam, as one Berliner to another, may I have your autograph?'. Dietrich agreed, signing 'From one Berliner to another — Marlene Dietrich'. It was one of the biggest thrills of Chris's life.

War of course meant lots of young men passing through Berlin. Chris fell for one of them, a nice chap in the Wehrmacht, or German Army. Borgia warned her, 'Be careful, get married or you'll be in trouble'. Chris certainly did not want to upset her parents, who had now moved to Berlin as well.

Chris took the advice, and after just six weeks of courtship in 1942 she became an army bride. The following year her first child, Harry, was born.

Her husband turned out not to be so nice after all. When he was home on leave he acted like a swine towards her, spending his time with other women. Chris could stand no more of this, so she put in for divorce and custody of the baby. Her husband was later taken prisoner of war by the Americans.

By the time Harry was born the music on the radio was more solemn, as news of defeats were broadcast, couched in the terms of heroic, strategic withdrawals, except people realised that the encircled Sixth Army could not withdraw any farther once they were encircled at Stalingrad. Berlin was now being regularly bombed by the Allies.

It was also dawning on folk that the Nazi regime left a lot to be desired in its treatment of some of its subjects. Chris remember an incident in a park when she offered some milk to a woman, as it was obvious that her baby was starving. The woman was wearing the yellow Star of David. A policeman came over and rebuked Chris for offering help to a sub-human. Chris did wonder about the fairness of labelling perfectly normal looking and acting people sub-human because they were Jewish.

The bombings and demands of total war began to take their toll on Berlin. Chris would take the pram that Harry was now too big for out onto the streets to fetch home coal to keep them both warm. At other times she would go to collect their meagre rations from the grocery shop around the corner from the apartment she now lived in. As she came back she would pass the unfortunates that war had left homeless in the streets, such as the ragged Ukrainians who found themselves over a thousand kilometres from their homeland, cold and hungry, doomed by choosing to fight their Russian oppressors from under the swastika. When the Red Army arrive they would either be shot there and there or be taken home to endure God knows what atrocities. Chris took pity on them and gave them some of the bread she could not afford to give.

In return, one of the men offered to help her with the fuel briquettes she was taking home. All the time this was happening, Chris noticed a woman, who had been watching Chris giving bread. The woman continued to look at her. Cradled in her rag covered arms was a baby, it was about the same age as Harry. Chris wanted to help, but was afraid to be seen giving help to a person she noticed was wearing a Jewish star. The authorities and informers might be watching.

Chris's compassion overcame her fear, and she told the woman to follow her to her flat, which was on the first floor of the block. it was what was known as a 'garden house', since it faced into a central courtyard with a garden in the middle. This meant it was not so easy for prying eyes from outside to see Chris and the woman enter, as all such flats had their entrances in the courtyard, and not outside in the street.

Once inside, Chris poured some milk into a cup for the baby, The woman gave the baby just a mouthful of milk, Chris went out to the front and back again, to keep watch. The woman gave Chris the cub back, it was empty, nothing was said. Chris wanted to cry, so painful was the need to say something to the woman, but neither of them spoke, you never knew who might be passing or listening just round the corner.

Chris saw plenty more like that woman hanging around, helpless, in the public parks, unable to sit on the seats marked, 'Nicht für Juden'.

Then Chris and Harry were bombed out by a morning air raid. She and Harry were safe in the shelter, but the flats were destroyed. She would have to build her life again and carry on.

However, not all the air raids proved so dangerous; small parachutes dropped out of the sky one day with leaflets in German attached. Chris watched them fall, and filled with curiosity watched them land. A woman told Chris not to pick any of them up, 'They are poison', she assured her.

Chris went to live in her mother's old flat, her father had got a commissionaire's job at the Reichstag apartments, and a flat came with the job.

Most days Chris would go out walking with the pram, or take the tram, which had a bigger compartment at one end for prams, and make the journey to see her mother at Knightszeplatz. One day Chris went to her mother's flat, and put baby Harry in bed, outside she could hear someone calling 'bambino, bambino'. It was a young Italian man who had been keeping the boiler going above the offices in the block. Chris was scared of him at first, but his outcry was purely because he had not seen a baby in ages.

Then the Dreher's were bombed out at the Reichstag apartments, the phosphorous bombs that did the damage re-igniting in a strange luminescence when it rained afterwards, futilely burning the remains of the destroyed flats.

Chris's parents were re-housed somehow, before the Russians arrived, when the Drehers took to hiding in cellars, not daring to venture out, for fear of the dreadful things that were being wrought in the name of the Allied victory outside: people eating dead animals in the street, no electricity or water. Like many others, they had to sell all their belongings for food. Harry had grown out of his pram, and needed feeding and clothing — how, Chris did not know. Eventually the Americans and British arrived. Hitler's dream had become a nightmare, and all Berliners were having to endure it over and over again with the coming of each day. But people are resilient and life went on.

The day that she met me, Chris was out with Harry and Lydia, a friend. Lydia, who could speak English, was the daughter of an old Berlin family, and had been educated at a private school. She lived across the road from Chris, and her mother lived above Chris, so they used to call across to one another from the balconies.

Chris and Lydia were on their way home by train, there was snow everywhere. They stopped at Reichschancellorplatz terminal, where they got off their train to continue on the underground Chris did not want to go onto the underground station platform because of all the soldiers hanging about, wolf whistling at all the young women, but Lydia lapped all this sort of attention up.

So they went onto the platform, and two British soldiers approached. I came up and took Harry's hand and started to make him repeat English phrases, Chris, a married woman still, did not know where to look. There was a 'non-frat' ban, soldiers were forbidden to speak to German civilians. Everyone seemed to be looking.

Chris told Lydia to ignore the soldier, but she was glad when they followed. Apparently it was Joe's eyes that did it, they were so black, and seemed to look right through her. 'Never had I seen such handsome eyes', she still says. 'You're a gypsy, eine Schwartz sie goine', she told me quite early on.

In the end my persistence paid off, because Lydia said that she would not go out with O'Keeve unless they made it a foursome. Chris was very uneasy about the situation. We went to see that Deanna Durbin film at the picture palace, where I spent the whole time telling Chris that I was going to marry her. She replied, 'Oh yeah?' Then she went back to Lydia's place in a rush, because of the curfew on civilians.

On another date, Chris was presented with some flowers. She thought how lovely they were until she realised that I had removed them from the local cemetery.

Then came the time for fusilier Morgan to go back to his unit. She later received a letter from me which Lydia read for her, which told her that I was coming to see her in another six weeks, which would be about the end of January. It was just after Christmas, there was a knock at the door to Chris's flat, it was open, it had been since the day the Russian troops had busted it. A voice shouted out, 'It's me, Eddie'. Chris said, 'I don't know an Eddie'. 'It's me, it's Joe.' 'I don't know a Joe.' 'It's Ted.' 'Oh, I know a Ted.' My cageyness with my own name had meant that Chris only knew me as 'Ted' or 'Smokey'!

I waltzed in, picked some mistletoe off of the wall, held it over Chris and confidently announced that next year we would be in England, and that we would be married. She tried to go and do her washing up, feigning indifference, but as she walked past me, I grabbed hold of her, nobody had been so passionate with her for a long time. She had missed me in the intervening months.

Then I had to meet the parents, with Lydia doing the translating. I was surprised to see that the Germans were an ordinary people much like the British. Later on, Dick Crossman told me that as Assistant Chief of the Psychological Warfare Division at SHAEF, he had been involved in the propaganda effort during the War; devoting his time to making films depicting the Germans as inhuman animals, or showing the Royal family visiting somewhere they were not actually at. Certainly these films succeeded in making the average squaddie believe that the enemy were a nation of square-headed, unfeeling brutes. I was not the only one to be surprised at the ordinariness of the Master Race. My interview passed by okay, although I'm not sure how much we all understood one another, but in any case, the time soon came round for me to go back to my unit again.

I took Chris to cinemas and dances, but would get drunk and often end up in a fight with anyone who so much as looked at Chris. Saturday night was not complete unless I was in a punch-up. Yet she put up with me and my antics.

Chris could not believe how ill I looked when she saw me after my release from prison. I then stayed with her for a whole week. After that, it was a case of her coming to stay with me, and here she was, in Britain, the land fit for heroes.

So for the next three years we lived in that one upstairs room, with only the noise of my brothers staggering vocally back from the pub late at night to serenade us to sleep. Things were so bad to start with that Chris often wished that she was back in Germany. She even felt guilty when I took her along to Barney Jacob's, to place a bet; she was hardly able to look him in the eye, as if she were personally responsible for the holocaust and all that had happened to his fellow Jews at Hitler's hands.

Poor little Harry was so badly undernourished when he arrived in Canning Town that we had to let him go into a convalescence home. We telephoned the home every single day of the six weeks that he was in there, even though we barely had two coppers to rub together. I was determined to keep in constant touch with my new son, determined to show him he now had a father who loved him. When we went to meet him from the coach that brought him back, I took him and put him on my shoulders, telling him that I would not let anyone take him away from us again.

In those early days of marriage, the first couple outside the family that we befriended were Ted and Cathy Stewardson. He was a working class intellectual, although he probably never saw himself in that light. It was his ideas on the lives, needs and problems of ordinary folk that influenced and added to my own thoughts, which Moggy had first planted in my mind. Certainly Cathy was the first person to make friends with Chris when they worked together. Ted himself was a bricklayer who I came across on the building sites.

Ted was a strong trade unionist, and it was evident from his eloquence and knowledge that he was head and shoulders above his workmates in thinking terms. I think that I subconsciously used him as my ideal working class man, a figure who represented what ordinary people could all be, given the chance. He was also a committed Catholic, unlike myself, although I was to use my contacts in the church to political ends.

He probably thought I was not really listening to his little five and ten minute chats in the cold, damp, dirty site canteens, but I absorbed his ideas as blotting paper absorbs ink. When I seemed to be paying him little attention I was in fact listening to his ideas and suggestions. It was he who first pointed me in the direction of the union-run Ruskin College. My later studies with the Ruskin stood me in good stead for my council and social work careers.

Chris managed to get a job working in a factory that made sweets. Even this proved hard going, as the other women workers proved to be difficult to get on with, so any hopes of building up work friendships quickly disappeared. Chris did not understand the unwritten rule amongst the other women, the one that said you did as little as possible for as much as possible. Her hard-working attitude, coupled with language difficulties meant that she was often a lonely figure who sat in the corner at break times. She even asked the line forelady if she should be working so hard; she was told to do what she thought was right.

Slowly, but very slowly, she became accepted, but only just.

There was one bright patch though, she struck up a friendship with another woman who was something of an outsider, someone who also sat alone. This turned out to be Cathy Stewardson. She originally came from Blackpool, so it is not difficult to imagine that perhaps her feelings were similar to those of the other non- cockney on the production line. This new-found friendship gave Chris more confidence in dealing with the routine of life in her adopted country.

At the work's Christmas party, everyone began to sing, 'Dear old pals, jolly old pals'. Chris tried to join in, thinking the words were 'Dear old cows, jolly old cows'! A man came over and asked her what words she was singing, when Chris discovered her mistake, she was genuinely surprised and embarrassed. She need not have been — the man was Cathy's husband, Ted. He soon made her feel at ease with his friendly manner.

It was not long before we were meeting the Stewardsons outside of our work, away from the less than matey surroundings of the sweet factory.

Things gradually improved for Chris at work. The people were becoming much more friendly, and my sister worked alongside as well. There was even the bonus of taking home and selling the odd Easter egg that the girls were making. They would put them in their bags and sell them for a shilling each, thus affording them enough for little luxuries such as a night out or birthday presents.

Even so, Chris was normally out of pocket before pay day on a Friday. It was known for me to borrow £1 from Mum to go down to Charlton dog track for the night. On one such visit with Chris in tow she picked six dogs just by their names, all of them won, so we ended up celebrating with a fish supper washed down with a couple of drinks at the pub. These small pleasures were relished amongst the day to day austerity of rationing and ration queues, such as that for the butcher's where Chris learnt much of her improving English.

The War had cost the whole country dear, not just in terms of lives lost, but also the repayments on the huge loan from the Americans, something we were destined to pay back for years. We had come out of the War poorer than we went in, having given everything; America had come out richer than ever, much to the resentment of ex-servicemen like myself and others. During the War American troops were largely viewed with contempt, British Tommies only really wanting the equipment they brought with them. Differences in pay did not help either, the £6 a week the Yanks enjoyed compared far too favourably with the miserable 7/- untrained, and derisory 14/- when fully trained that the British private received. This only emphasised the relative wealth of our two nations. It also meant that women flocked to the G.I.s, with their glamorous uniforms and cash to treat a girl properly.

We also considered them a liability in battle; in the years after the War, my brother-in-law, Carl, would remark to me that 'our' Americans were like 'their' (Germany's) Italians. In Berlin I had spoken with a captured Wehrmacht officer, who said that his army kept three times as many soldiers opposite a British division as they did an American one.

Even the transatlantic attitude to military life appalled me. I might have been a rebel, but even I would not have dreamed of swearing at an officer during conversation in the manner I over-heard from a USAAF private at an air base in Suffolk; their casual-ness defied belief.

Anyway, at that stage of things it was a case of could not live with them, could not live without them.

The other set of people who annoyed me to a similar degree were my bosses. I just could not hold a job down for very long. Sooner or later my temper would get the better of me, and some arch remark from my foreman would be enough for me to either floor him on the spot or down tools and walk off. I knew I needed work to keep my family together, but I was damned if I was going to let anyone treat me like dirt, I was not under King's Regulations any more.

Chris kept working hard, never giving in to the difficulties we faced. Even when we fell out with Mum over the amount of noise she said we made, and I decided to move out rather than put up with the arguments, Chris still stuck with me. We could not afford to rent anywhere from a private landlord, and the West Ham council list seemed as long as the Great Wall of China (over 20,000 strong, in fact) so we ended up at a hostel called Langthorne House, in Leytonstone.

Whilst we were there, Chris became very ill. A doctor came to see her, and dismissed her pain as gastroenteritis. Then Chris got much worse. I called to fetch the doctor out again; he promised to visit, but failed to show. When I got back from work and he had still not turned up, I decided to call an ambulance. Chris was taken to hos-pital with what turned out to be a burst appendix. I stayed all night by the telephone, but she pulled through — illustrating in one go the best and worst of the new National Health Service. Again things do not seem to change too much in some respects.

Soon after, Chris announced that she was going back to work, the next day she did. I thought it was far too quick, but she was a fighter. I think that is why my father got on so well with her.

Moggy seemed immortal to me, so I could not understand why one day in 1949 I was standing with the rest of the Morgan clan in his bedroom, waiting for him to die. As we stood around, talking quietly, hardly able to understand that he was now so ill and wasted that he would soon be gone, I began to think back to all the crazy things this wonderful character had done.

One day he got very drunk, 'I'm going back to sea,' he announced. He was quite old by then, but he packed his bag and set off towards the docks. Mum started crying, but I told her 'Don't worry Mum, he'll get to the nearest pub and he'll get as pissed as a lord, and then someone will bring him home to you tonight'. And that was a certainty, because that was what always happened.

He could be as soft as anything, but that did not make him any less hard when necessary. When he was in his fifties he was attacked in the street by a couple of yobbos. Moggy laid one of them out and sent the other running, which is lucky for the yob, because five minutes afterwards I came round the corner with some of my brothers. If he had still been there and standing, we would have done more than seen him off.

These and other times went though my thoughts as I looked down at the figure on the bed. Then the whole family suddenly stopped talking all at once. Moggy sat up, and it seemed as though all the pain had gone from his face. Then he spoke:

'There's a good boy, Harry Boy, you found my tobacco tin.'

He was referring to a tin he had lost some twenty years before, when my brother Harry was still alive. Moggy had sent him to look for it, but he came back crying because he could not find it. But Moggy still gave him a sixpence for trying. A little while afterwards Harry died.

Having spoken, Moggy lay back, quite contented.

'Look, he's breathing better,' I told the rest of the family. Sure enough, for a few seconds, the wheezing that had plagued nearly half his life was gone. Then he died. I went berserk, screaming:

'There ain't no fucking God, why take a man like him?

Chris and the others could not quieten me. The whole family had idolise him, we were all shattered. He was barely 60 years old.

His funeral was the biggest ever seen in Canning Town. His old employer, Barney Jacobs, King of the Whitechapel bookmakers, sent a wreath of flowers that covered the entire hearse. The flowers were arranged in the shape of a football pitch, in the middle of which was a football of claret and light blue, the colours of West Ham. in

smaller flowers across the football was the legend 'From one sports-
man to another — B.J.'.

Crowds lined the streets as the procession came towards the
Beckton Arms. Coppers stood there saluting, and I thought what
corrupt bastards they were, they had taken so much money from
him, and now they stood there saluting as though butter would not
melt in their mouths — hypocrites. People just stood there and
cried. I realised just how much this local character meant to everyone, and how much affection people had for him.

Chris was also shaken by Moggy's passing; he had become a mainstay in her life. When I shouted, argued and treated her badly, it was
Moggy who would comfort Chris, telling her 'Don't worry girl, he'll
grow out of it. All men do. He'll turn out to be a good husband.
Don't worry, just stick by him.'

I could hardly hold back the tears, but the memories he left with
me are eternal. Thinking back now makes me realise the importance
of a father being close to this children, perhaps this is where I have
gone wrong. All my life was given to politics while my children were
growing up, and now I wonder why my son is not closer to me.
Perhaps because the politics did not let me be close to him. That is
why I try to make it up to my grandchildren now. All the love I get
from them repays every little bit of affection I have shown them.
Thank you Moggy.

Mum never married again, remaining a widow for the last 30
years of her life. Twelve months or so after my father's death, she
found a male friend who would meet her in the pub for a drink.
The rest of the family frowned on this. We all made it quite clear
that as far as we were concerned, nobody would ever replace our
father. Right or wrong, that is how strongly Moggy's presence
remained.

Mum got a job at a nearby hospital, where she spent years
scrubbing and polishing.

Years later I was by her death bed, I looked down and kissed her,
saying out loud 'What a hard time you had, bringing up a family'.

Ours was four times the size of a modern family, there were no
washing machines, freezers or microwave ovens. Yet she managed.
Each morning she would scrub the front step at home until it was
milk white. She took great pride in her step. All she had known
throughout her time was hardship and poverty. All she had asked
for was to be able to look after her husband and her children, and
to enjoy the odd glass of Guinness down the pub on a Saturday
night.

Thinking of her life made me muse about the old days and the
lives people had to live. Who really helped them? The Tories? Not a

chance. Even the Labour Party had betrayed them. I have been right to the top in local politics, but even my enthusiasm has been swamped with disillusionment when I have seen how councillors have treated the people. Corruption in both major parties was and is just as bad, but what can you expect when there are men and women 'serving' on local councils who are not fit for the job. I have known that since the the the day I tried to get Chris, Harry and myself out of that hostel in Leytonstone, and into a council house.

Week after week I went to the housing department, demanding to know where I was on the housing list. I would go to the Labour councillors over in West Ham, never thinking to ask any of the Tories. My personal calls often in me being insulted, one man slamming the door in my face as he said 'Don't you dare come to my house of a nighttime, you write me a letter'. I knew if I did write I would be ignored, so how else was I to contact those who were supposed to represent my interests, unless I saw them face to face in the evenings — I could hardly afford or expect to get time off work, I needed to hang on to a job.

Then I realised that if I wanted to beat their system, I would have to learn just how it worked. I studied the housing points system, working out how many points our situation entitled us to. Then I would find myself reading reports in the local press, explaining how the council's housing programme was romping ahead, as people with as few as 65 points were being housed. I knew this to be little more than propaganda to keep everyone quiet.

I bided my time, until the chairman of housing made an official press statement to the effect that the Labour council had housed families with 65 points. I marched into the housing department, newspaper in hand, and demanded to know why if the press release was true, my family was still waiting to be housed, when we had 70 points on the housing system.

'It's nothing to do with you,' the woman on the front desk told me.

'Look 'ere love, you either speak to me, or I'll go to the newspapers, and you can speak to them. I think you people are on the fiddle; I think you're taking money.'

I had learnt the art of blackmail through fear, and this was to remain a tool of mine during my political career. I was able to instil fear into fellow councillors and administrators alike, always forcing them to back down or come around to my way of thinking on a particular matter. I have always believed that everyone has something to hide.

I could immediately sense that I had hit a nerve when I mentioned bribery to the woman. She ushered me into another room to see the senior administration officer. He started to warn me about making accusations.

'Well then, we'll let the newspapers decide. All I'm telling you is what's in this paper, and I've got 70 points, so why aren't I housed? Either this bloke in the paper is a bloody liar, or there's a fiddle going on with you people. Now I don't care which way it is.'

At that stage I had not yet understood that it is better to make an attack without swearing. I was still in greater fear of these people than I made out, but I had been quick to realise that you do not show that you are frightened.

The officer told me that I would hear more of the matter, and the council would probably take action against me.

'That's up to you mate, that's entirely up to you, but if I don't hear from you about a house within a week I'm going to the newspapers; I'm going to the 'Stratford Express'.'

Two days later I received a letter offering me a flat in Stratford. My suspicions about corruption in the West Ham housing department seemed correct, they were afraid of the press. In years to come I would be proved right; in the meantime I had beaten them.

Chris and I were overjoyed that we had somewhere we could call 'home' again. The flat we were promised had been 'requisitioned', we were told, and was in a seedy part of Stratford, but none of this worried up. 'We'll do it up ourselves,' I told Chris.

She worked hard when we moved in, so it was not long before the place looked comfortable and felt respectable. I now knew that more than ever I must hold down a regular job, otherwise our rent would end up in arrears.

We had to share a toilet with a middle-aged woman who lived downstairs. She came up to welcome us. Her breath reeked of whisky, so much so that I had to turn my head away. We soon noticed that it was her habit to bring a lot of different men home: I often wondered if she was on the game, but at first I did not give a damn how she earned the rent.

At least I did not give a damn until one day Harry came up from the toilet with his trousers soaking wet with urine, because whoever had been in there before him had splashed all over the seat without cleaning up. I rushed downstairs and forced the woman's door open. There she was with yet another 'boyfriend'. I grabbed and pushed him out of the door, continuously punching him as I forced him onto the street. Then I went back inside.

'You dirty old whore. If ever my son comes up like that again, I'll push your bleedin' face down that toilet.

A few days followed before a letter came informing me that she had complained to the council. I paid another personal visit to the housing department, even though it meant having to grovel for time off work, and again I gave them the benefit of my opinion.

'I think you purposely gave me a flat, knowing that old boot lived there, just to get revenge for what I said to you,' I told the officer.

He did not reply at first, but just grinned, that told me I was right.

'We've got nothing else to offer you, that's all there is. The waiting list for new places is so long that it'll be at least 20 years before you can think about it. The only chance you'll get is if you go to a New Town.'

'You can stick your New Town up your arse.'

I walked away. I knew they had me over a barrel. Strictly speaking, they had housed me. It would be impossible to prove that they had purposely put us above the prostitute. I was not about to leave the East End and live in one of the government spawned New Towns they were building.

If you can't beat 'em, join 'em. So the old saying goes. I joined the Labour Party. I did not take much interest at first, just going to a few meetings, watching and listening. As I heard the councillors speaking, it became transparent that they were crooked, even though they were supposed to be fighting for the social revolution.

I went to speak to a couple of them about the possibility of getting a house exchange, but they all said they could not really help; they were unable to interfere with the housing list. 'Not much,' I thought. 'If it was one of your bleedin' family, you would soon move them'.

As time passed I started to get involved with union work. This meant always being amongst the first to get sacked if there was trouble or work was short on a job. Along with the other militants in the local building trade, I found it difficult to make ends meet — purely for standing up for decent treatment at work. Chris and I struggled through financially, somehow. We had our share of arguments, most of which she won, I'm now glad to say.

It was during these hard times that the woman downstairs would come up to our flat and sit with Chris for a while, then slip her a fiver, saying 'pay me back when you can'. I must admit that I found this touching, so much so that I relented in my opinion of her, telling myself that people could not always help what they were. She had risen above our row, so I had to do the same. But I still wanted out.

Then an event happened which backed my first impressions of our dubious neighbour: one day there was a street party going on outside the flats, to celebrate the Queen's coronation. Harry had gone back inside, but then came running out again. He came up to me, shouting 'Dad, the lady downstairs is with a man, an' they got no clothes on; they're playing gee-gees'.

I went mad. I ran back to the flats to find the woman in bed with another client. Terrified, they cowered as I looked at them. They need not have worried, this time I did not use my fists. 'You dirty bastards'.

That was all my disgust would allow me to say. Being on the game was one thing, but bringing men into the same building as that where my little son could not fail to notice what was going on, virtually flaunting the seedy goings-on in our faces, that was something else.

That something else was the final straw. If it was the only way I could bring the boy up somewhere decent, then I would leave the East End. I would have to eat my words and apply for a house in one of the New Towns.

We were granted a house in Basildon, one of the 15 New Towns being put up in a ring around London, in an effort to clear the slum conditions and overcrowding in the capital.

Chris, Harry and I joined the cockney exodus to the green countryside of Essex, where everything would be a land of milk and honey — or so I thought. After all, it had looked quite nice when I had gone there on holidays as a nipper. What is more, there would be plenty of building work going on, so my skills as a tiler would be constantly in demand, union firebrand or not. Yes, the more I thought about it, the better an idea it seemed to be. A new start in a new place with new attitudes. I would not have to put up with the old system any more. These New Towns were meant to be entirely different. So I armed myself with something akin to the Old West pioneering spirit, and set off towards the New East.

My life certainly ended up being entirely different from how it had been, but not in a way I could have imagined.

Chapter Seven
OLD WINE IN NEW BOTTLES

During the War, a plan to relieve London's East End of its squalor and overcrowding was put forward in what became known as the Abercrombie Plan, named after its originator. The plan called for Greater London to be ringed with fourteen new towns, which would absorb the population growth in the capital, and improve the lot of many people by providing them with a better standard of housing linked to planned industrial and commercial growth.

The 1945 Labour Government formally adopted this plan and passed the New Towns Act in April 1946. The then Minister of Town and Country Planning, Silkin, was charged with the responsibility of setting up these new utopias and spreading the gospel. One such New Town, as they were officially designated, was to be built around some towns and villages in South Essex. It would take its name from the village at the centre of the proposed development, a sleepy little place called Basildon.

Silkin addressed a local public meeting about the building of the town, and in an attempt to fire the enthusiasm of the people, he told them that one day people from all over the world would want to come and visit Basildon. He was to be proved right, for a while at least, but I doubt if many believed him that night.

Basildon New Town was composed of the towns of Pitsea, Billericay and Wickford, along with the more rural areas of Vange, Basildon, Laindon and Langdon Hills. The idea was sold to the locals on the basis of an area devoid of the muddy roads, lack of street lights and public amenities, such as shops.

I arrived to a Basildon full of dirty roads, devoid of street lights and with hardly a shop in sight. I had armed with the spirit of an Old West pioneer, and judging from the dirt and the number of cowboys who were running the place, it was just as well. This was Dodge City, not some marvellous piece of social planning come true.

When I first moved to Basildon in 1953 I had no big plans for me or my family. I was there purely because we had been offered an exchange by someone who could not stand the privations and the relative silence that the fledgeling New Town offered. People quickly looked for a place back and London. Chris and I went back to the East End every weekend desperately hoping to see a suitable exchange postcard in a newsagent's shop window.

But gradually we realised just how pleasant Basildon was after we returned from a weekend in filthy London. We grew to value the peace and relatively clean air, to enjoy looking out and not seeing mile after mile of grim slums and to walk out in the country which was on our doorstep. Yet conditions for the new inhabitants of Basildon were bad, and there were one or two unpleasant echoes from the past.

Lizzie, the old biddy we had tried to escape from, moved to Basildon soon after ourselves, unbeknown to us. The first we knew was when she hailed Chris in the street one day. She called out as she tried to pull a trolley along, battling against the obvious drunken stupor she was in.

'Is he still beating you?'

She was only joshing, but Chris was very embarrassed. The treatment we received from the powers that be, and the locals' open hostility towards us made life as deprived as any cockney back street, but without the compensation of East End camaraderie. People did not come and chat to you, or sit on their doorsteps. They were inside, the women using their new-fangled washing machines, the men perhaps watching the television if they could afford to rent or buy one. There were only two pubs in the area, 'The Bull' and 'The Barge', and precious little else to do at nights. Many people ended up at the doctors, suffering from New Town sickness.

It was like living in a ghetto. We had only one shop in our neighbourhood. As soon as you stepped inside and opened your mouth the shopkeeper would say 'you Londoners want to get back home'. But he still took our money. On another occasion I got on one of the buses that ran between the existing towns. I forget which, and all along the journey the conductress was telling the passengers how dirty the New Towners were, and how they had spoiled local life since they turned up. I could only stand to hear so much denigration of decent folk, so eventually I went for her, and was chucked off the bus for my troubles.

We had a local bus service in the New Town, it was run by a chap called Campbell, he was also the driver of the broken down old heap that passed for his bus. Chris would go over to Pitsea Broadway to do her shopping, and then hop on Campbell's bus, like everyone else who paid for the service, she was able to ask to be dropped off at their own front door. Yes he was virtually a taxi service. 'I live first on the left, second on the right', you would hear people say. There was just one small problem with Campbell, he was officially registered blind! Do not ask me how he got away with it for so long, but amazingly he did. He could of course see after a fashion, but his eyesight was totally inadequate for driving. Unfortunately he knocked someone down. The bus service was then switched to the rather more luxuriously maintained cream painted and green striped vehicles of Eastern National. They were not quite so accommodating in dropping people off, so strong boots were advisable for walking through the giant building site that was Basildon.

Chris and I would go to the pictures, at Hadleigh, eight miles away, and walk back. The last bus through Basildon ran at nine o'clock.

In addition there was no street lighting or any pavements. Industry consisted almost solely of the building trade, it was hoped new firms would be attracted to the area later on. I would look up some days at the place and think what a wilderness it was.

Because the area we lived in had not even existed before in council parish terms, there were no councillors to represent the new settlers of Basildon, so we were disenfranchised and alone against the Whitehall-run body that the Government had set up to administer the New Town housing and industrial development. This body was the Basildon Development Corporation (BDC), and instead of being an enlightened go-ahead group of professionals free of red-tape, they were a bunch of licensed gangsters who made the antics of the old East End landlords look tame by comparison.

The BDC were building 1,000+ houses a year in a good year, this was their main target, to build as quickly as possible, and blow how it was done. The rents that they charged were slightly higher than those charged by the local authority, the Billericay Urban District Council, but a lot higher than those we were used to in London. Mine was 12/- when I left London, but nearly half as much again, 17/4 (87p) in Basildon.

The New Town was still a country area paying country wages — about £3 a week lower than London. Everyone was living on Hire Purchase schemes as a result; we all hoped to kit our new homes out on HP and pay for it all scrap by scrap over the weeks.

Basildon Development Corporation rent collectors were the public face of authority, and they were swines. They would insult women on the doorstep when they complained about the state of their new houses, e.g. 'the ceiling is falling down' — as it often was. The rent collector would reply 'if you don't like it, then get back to the scum you've come from'. Many collectors were physically assaulted by husbands as a result, and this led to families being evicted on that basis.

Although the BDC houses were quite good compared to those I had known, they were far below the standards of the private housing being erected. Why is it that housing for the masses is always constructed on the basis of quickness and cheapness? In this case, the eagerness of the BDC to concrete and brick over the Essex countryside as fast as possible proved to be a false economy, as buildings began to show faults that cost dearly to put right.

'If you keep on complaining, you'll be out on the street with your husband and child' an official of the BDC warned Chris, on being told by her about how pulling our toilet chain caused the cistern to collapse. A neighbour complained that a sewer pipe had been plumbed through their larder and had burst. The BDC were not too interested in problems of that nature.

'The attitude of the BDC officials gave birth to the man who became the bane of their life — Joe Morgan'. Peter Lucas, a local journalist, wrote those words, and they are true. I helped to found a Barstable Tenants Association to protect the rights of all the New Towners in our area, and to give us a voice. Yet our association was not even recognised by BDC, the sort of arrogant approach that set the tone of all their dealings with the outside world and myself in particular.

As I have said, we had no amenities at first, and we asked for a hall to hold meetings and social functions in. Eventually the Corporation gave us a piece of land and said, 'build your own'. So we did, putting up a wooden hall in the evening after work at Louncies Road. I suppose they thought that we should have been grateful for the land, but we had saved them money and time putting up a meeting place that any large housing development is entitled to if it is to have any lifeblood at all. Episodes like this began to convince me that people could be mobilised to stand up for themselves, and do more than just stick two fingers up at society. I had taken the first step towards becoming a councillor.

The BDC continued to listen to no-one but Whitehall, and made some stupid near-sighted decisions. Later on, when I did go onto the council, I implored the BDC to build wider roads and leave room for garages in their new developments, as working class people would all soon have cars. This was scoffed at, and nowadays roads are still being widened at the tax payer's expense, as all New Towns were funded out of central government, not the local authorities' coffers.

In any case, the old Billericay Council were an ineffective body, who let the BDC ride roughshod over them, and who had not even organised their own services properly; even their workmen carried out jobs without the benefit of any municipal stores. Everything was bought locally at over-the-odds prices. What match were such an inefficient bunch for the Corporation? Change had to come from outside to stop an organisation that was not just arrogant and off-hand, but contained some people who were using the New Town as an opportunity to make money through selling development information.

Basildon literally was a shack development before the New Towns Act plucked it from obscurity. It was composed of the 'champagne plots' of the sort that I had visited as a boy on holiday in Vange. Many people had settled in these wooden chalets, bungalows and sheds after they had retired from work in London.

So here we had a largely old and by now impoverished group of people who had compulsory purchase orders placed on them by the BDC. The land needed to be cleared to have proper estates and factories built, that was fine in itself. Yet many of these folk were robbed by an estate agent, who always knew up to a year ahead of any proposed purchase orders. He would then make a derisory offer to the often frightened elderly people who lived in the bulldozer's path. He would tell them that their house would be flattened. 'I can get you a better price,' he would lie, preying on their fear, ignorance and poverty.

In one case, a Mrs Morgan (no relation), who was a widow of 80, lived alone in the shack her husband had built out of materials he had carried from the nearest railway station across the fields. I came to her as a councillor, she was in a state, weeping — she didn't know what to do. She did not want to sell, but if she had to, should she trust this estate agent? I went to the BDC and complained — the agent made a further offer of £600, I said no, and demanded to know how an estate agent was able to get prior knowledge of Corporation development plans. I asked to see the books, to find out how much the agent was selling the properties on for, but typically the BDC refused.

After questions in the House they had to relent, and showed me accounts that revealed they were paying £1,400 per property from the agent. Somebody in the BDC was getting a backhander from him. I had only uncovered this improper use of information by enlisting the help of Labour M.P.s, otherwise all those concerned would have got away with it.

In the early days of Basildon I tried to ask Sir Bernard Braine, the original M.P. for the constituency that included the New Town area, a question at a meeting held at 'The Barge'. I stood on a stool to be seen, and asked if he would look into the way BDC was treating London folk. He did not know me at the time, but replied 'Get back to London'.

I was no communist, but I did stand up for my rights as a worker, and those of others in my trade. I was given my first job in the area with W.C. French, the biggest building contractor in the town. I organised the workforce into a union, still being a paid-up member of the TGWU. All the Londoners in the building trade had a union background.

I was a labourer to start with. After about 18 months the work on our site finished. This proved a good excuse to get rid of me. Unions upheld workers rights and were concerned about quality and safety on site, this ran against the contractual aims of work handed out to building firms in the BDC. I was a little red pain in the backside, so I had to go.

Then I worked for another builder, and again I organised a union shop. We struck over poor working conditions, and so I was sacked. After some more jobs I became almost unemployable. Some foremen were honest enough to tell me why, but I always knew that my work ability was not at issue. Times were soon hard for my family, but through it all Chris stuck by me.

I was excluded from work, on the dole. I was advised to leave town to find work, but I told them that nobody was forcing me out of Basildon. Then why not get work outside of town, it was queried? No, it was a matter of principle that the cowboys were not going to run me out of town, I was not taking the next stage out.

Later I was very fortunate to be taken on by a small firm at Wickford, run by a chap called Bibby, who knew that his outfit was too small to be organised, so I was no threat to him. Everyone there treated me properly anyway. But I still paid my union dues.

Sir Richard Bonilack owned one of the few factories in the New Town, and was also on the Board of BDC, the executive body that was all powerful, and composed of a very narrow section of society. Sir Richard was President of the Basildon Golf Society and was a typical Board member. His factory, which manufactured specialist car bodies, went on strike. The BDC threatened to evict any of Bonilack's workers who were their tenants for striking, as they realised that non-payment of rent would be an easy lever to get their own way. I called the building workers out in sympathy and against the BDC, but received no help from elsewhere, as the Tories and their fellow travellers on Billericay Council just stood by and let blackmail take its inevitable course.

These were hard times for the Morgans. Often we did not have enough food to eat, or even any coal for the fire. Then Harry and I would go up to the railway line and pick up scraps of coal that had fallen off the steam engines.

Towards the end of most weeks all that was left in the house was a couple of potatoes, and these would be made into chips for Harry whilst Chris and I went without.

'What are you eating Mum, Dad?'

'Oh, we've had ours son, you eat yours.'

Chris found a job, and she worked hard, backing me 100 per cent in all I did. Even Harry realised things were really bad. He had a paper round, and time and time and time again he would thrust me a couple of pounds, saying 'you pay me back when you get it'.

I even went and found some work on the railway lines, working all night unloading trucks of ballast. It was back breaking work, and reminded me of Moggy shovelling away at Beckton gas works. Many men went there and found they could not stick the pace, working alongside the Irish navvies. They would last an hour or two, and then have to pack in, with not a penny to show for their efforts. The ganger probably pocketed what they were owed. I stuck it out, I was still young, and as strong as a lion. I could match the navvies shovel for shovel, and at the end of a night's work I had a fiver to show for my efforts. And that was quite a bit of money in the mid-'fifties. Then the Morgans would have feast royals. There would be presents for Harry and a few little treats, and life would not seem so bad after all.

But this work was not regular, and our finances became so perilous that we were in danger of being evicted for non-payment of rent. I swallowed my pride and went to see the Deputy Housing Manager, a Mr Kent. Knowing I would get short shrift from him in his office, I decided to wait outside the church where he was a lay preacher, in the hope that I could reason with him face to face, and he would overturn an eviction decision.

He came out, and when I tried to talk to him, he scathingly told me to clear off.

'Don't you dare come near me on a Sunday, if you want to see me come to my office. And don't bother me if you've no money to pay the arrears.'

I looked at him and swore that one day I would pay him back for talking to me in that fashion. When I became a councillor, people would turn up at my house at all hours, weekends included. I did not turn them away or abuse them. I made sure that I would not forget Kent's treatment of me, and some years later, after I had avoided being evicted by scraping enough rent together from God knows where, I had my chance to put the record straight.

A reception was being held for me, 'The Father of Basildon' as the press had christened me. The Corporation Officers were being presented to me, and Kent was among them. He came towards me.

'Get this man away from me, I have no wish to associate with him,' I informed the whole room at the top of my voice.

Apart from my language, it was the venom in my voice that shocked everyone. They all fell silent. Kent was ushered out of the room. I turned to the Corporation's General Manager, Charles Boniface, and told him that filth like that was not even fit to work in local government. I related what had happened years before.

'You should have come to me.'

'You must be joking, you wouldn't see me, you wouldn't even open the door to me.'

I turned on my heel and walked out, leaving them standing there with their glasses of wine and champagne. As I reached the door I turned to bid them farewell.

'You can stick that champagne and all your sandwiches right up your arses, the lot of you.'

I left. I can remember that day vividly, I make no apologies for it, and still relish the memory of the Corporation's collective faces.

Employers exploited the building workers, when it rained you stopped work and went home without pay immediately. Normally, in London, it had to rain for quite a length of time before work was called off. The same happened at the first sign of winter frosts. Many of these BDC contractors were as corrupt as any Chicago gangsters, lining their own pockets, but it was difficult to prove.

As a councillor I later had an opportunity to prove my point. In 1960 some concrete pre-fabricated houses were being built in Kent View Road to a wooden frame design called 'Bardfield'. Concrete was poured into the wooden shell blocks, creating walls which were supposed to be reinforced with steel. The site foreman tipped me off that the site Corporation Officer was selling the steel back to the lorry driver who delivered it. He was then passing a share onto Corporation officers before putting the rest in his own pocket. At first I did not believe these allegations.

The houses were completed during October and November, and were ready for letting by December. They were not let immediately because of the season. During Christmas they fell down, but fortunately they were still empty. I asked Dame Evelyn Sharp, the Local Government Permanent Secretary, for an enquiry, because I knew if I went to the BDC they would cover up. To my amazement, the Dame said no. She was advised there was corruption going on, but was desperate to protect one of her 'babies', the BDC. It also transpired that a relative of hers was serving in the hierarchy of the BDC. I now realised that Whitehall could not be trusted either. The scale and the spread of the corruption was far bigger than I had first imagined. I was determined that the builder would not work in Basildon, again, because I reckoned they had a hand in all of this.

But it was not just houses, on another occasion I saw some soft-fibre pipes being laid for a mains sewer. I was told to mind my own business by the Corporation. Of course the pipes later collapsed, and had to be dug up. Somebody had supplied those as proper sewage pipes and kept the difference, there is no doubt of that.

I was a thorn in the side of the BDC from the start. When I first became a councillor I would ring the BDC up and they would say 'I don't want to speak to you', and put the telephone down.

The BDC was composed of civil servants appointed by central government, the formidable Dame Evelyn Sharp being their boss in Whitehall. The Board was composed of ex-army officer types like Brigadier Knapton, late of the Royal Engineers, who once charmingly informed me that 'I'd have had you thrashed in the Army!' this when I was a councillor. BDC headquarters, the vipers' nest, was at Gifford House in Pitsea. If I was going to take this bunch on, I needed more weaponry, so I went ahead and took a Trades Union correspondence scholarship from Ruskin College.

I studied Industrial Law and Social Studies. They fuelled my later desire to do social work. My teacher was amazed at the writings in my essays. When I did have to travel up to Ruskin to do some class work, she told me she was fascinated by my grasp of social problems, saying that it was streets ahead of the work done by my contemporaries. I managed to obtain a certificate in both subjects, but I found the law side hard; I had to go into the library just to look up words being used. I felt at a disadvantage on the course at the start, but with encouragement I studied at home and felt ready to take on the pig-headed BDC.

I had joined the local Labour Party after about nine months in town, knowing that it was the only way to fight. I planned to get on to Billericay Council and take on the system. Bill Ferrier, a party collector, first introduced me into the Party, I knew him from working together on the building sites, and in any case, his father was a big figure in the East End.

Bill wanted to form a Basildon Labour Party, distinct from the old mob in Billericay, formed of councillors such as farmer Kay, Harry Tanswell and a couple of elderly people. In common with other locals, they did not like New Towners, comrades or not, and were not going to let go of power to newcomers. We had a third ally in Alf Dove, who was Chairman of our ward in Barstable. Alf was the manager of the local Co-op store, which had at last given us somewhere friendly to shop. He was a nice chap, and like us was determined to help the ordinary folk on the estates. I eventually succeeded him as ward Chairman. George Elder was another ally, he became Chairman of the ward in the 1960s, when Alf and I moved onto the Council.

I used to have to walk to the meetings at the Council chamber in Billericay. On the way back home, the Tories would drive by in their cars, laughing and hooting at me, waving with just two unfriendly fingers. I did not give a damn. What did hurt was when other Labour councillors drove by and never offered me a lift. I lost count of how many times I walked home from Billericay, and sometimes it was two or three in the morning before I walked through the door.

The people of the old Billericay Labour Party were anti-Tory, but not socialist. To them it was all parish pump politics. The first time there was a selection for councillors in the party after I had joined, a load of old dears in wheelchairs were brought to the meeting, it all looked like an old people's home had been emptied for the day. Then they were told when to vote by their bosses in the Old Guard.

In 1955 I asked for selection to go onto the panel of Council candidates, but not surprisingly I was turned down. Eventually we Londoners overran the ancients with numbers. They were nice enough people who were for Labour but did not understand the movement. Somehow they had achieved control by the mid-'fifties, with Harry Tanswell as Chairman in 1956. This should have been the chance for Basildon to move forward but they missed the boat. It was up to the next generation to take the bull by the horns.

I started in the Party as a ward collector, collecting 1/6d (7^1/2p) a quarter subs, i.e. I would spread the load by taking 6d a month from my ward's members. In this way I soon got to know people and people got to know me. I quickly built up membership in my ward. Our ward's numbers were up to 350, more than the whole of the the modern day Basildon Labour Party.

I started organising dances and children's parties for ward members. Another Labour man, Johnny Blake, had a jazz band, which he would get on the back of a lorry on a Sunday morning and we would have a cavalcade through the streets. People would turn out to clap and cheer.

At last the New Town was allocated some seats on an enlarged council, to recognise the growth of Basildon. Alf Dove, myself and some others were asked if we wished to be nominated. I was selected to represent my own ward. On the day of the election, my ward's returning officer was amazed, instead of the normal council vote of a few hundred, I got 4,200 odd votes, while the Tory had polled just 80. Joe Morgan was on Billericay Urban District Council, 1956, along with Alf and the growing numbers of the fledgeling Basildon Labour Party.

This meant an end to the parish pump and episodes in the council such as that of Basildon's own 'Clochmerle'. Just in the French village of Clochmerle, so in rural Essex the building of a public toilet caused a storm in a chamber pot. The old Labour mob opposed it being built, because they thought the siting unsuitable. When a Labour councillor got the council to site it at the bottom part of his back garden, for which he was paid £50, the Labour Group suddenly supported this 'improved' siting.

On my first day in the council chamber, a couple of old councillors came up and told me to sit and listen and not to speak for at least nine months, because I would get mixed up and the Tories would tear me to pieces. I sat still and silent like a good boy for a whole 20 minutes. Then the subject of council house building came up. Labour councillors were agreeing with Tories that people did not really need council houses. Twenty were quite enough to build in a year. They thought that it would do these people good to live at home with their parents for a while, after all, they were not really not old enough to be married anyway. I got up and blasted the Labour councillors.

'Why don't you go over there and sit with that bloody crowd?'

There was a banging of the gavel.

'Who is that man?'

'Shut him up.'

I was ordered out of the council chamber — at that stage I did not know how to use the system yet. In later meetings I would make sure press knew I was going to be thrown out and make sure that the police had to bodily lift me from chamber. At first I would walk into the meetings with notes, but I soon had to tear them up, I just could not rehearse being blunt or insulting.

The Treasurer of the Council, Lofty Cousins, owned a couple of antique shops in Billericay. One day soon after I had started on the Council he came out to the toilet where I was cooling off after another argumentative session and said 'You're going to go a long way on this council'.

'Thanks.'

'But always remember something.'

'What's that?'

'Follow me.'

Then he took me into the Council rest room, and took three forks and said 'See that fork, that fork and that fork. They're exactly the same, and they all cost the same, same quality, so why did that cutlery company get the contract to supply?'

'Cheapest?' I naïvely ventured.

'No, they all cost exactly the same to make and sell.'

'I don't know,' I replied, still a bit naïve.

'A councillor pushes one of these forks, telling you this is the one you should buy, pushes it like mad. Now there's only one reason he's pushing and that's because someone's going to give him a drink for doing it. Bear that in mind, boy, and use it.

'Put the fear of god into the one who's trying to make you give a contract, or buy something when there's no earthly reason why you couldn't buy the same product elsewhere.'

I never forgot that and indeed rooted out a lot of corruption, though I did not make myself too popular with some sections of the Council by doing so.

Lofty was also right about me on the Council, I became the spokesman of the Left-wing in the Party. Gradually we became the majority, and I took control of the Party.

The Left did not gain power without some bitter fighting that took place in and outside the Council Chamber in 1961. The Party and Council Group were bitterly split between Left and Right. One of the main disputes was civil defence, with those of us on the Left refusing to co-operate with the Government and by now Tory-controlled Council. Alf Dove felt so strongly about this that he came out of his normal neutrality and resigned from the Group whip and sat as an independent for about six months when I led the Left to victory in the battle to disassociate ourselves from the whole concept of civil defence.

I gave out the press information on a so called nerve centre where all emergency meals and decisions would be taken in event of war. No-one in the Civil Defence had been told that the place had been demolished nine months previously. I was threatened with legal action by the Council under the Official Secrets Act, but as was usual by this time I ignored them and went ahead. The press had a field day.

Other issues the Labour Group were split on included direct labour for the Council, the closed shop, no evictions for rent, no co-operation with BDC and full control over council staff, all of which the Left were for and the Right were not.

In 1962 I had my chance to kill-off the threat of the Right when there were fresh Leadership elections. I stood against the Right's candidate, Ron Rice, and won. After that I was unopposed for Leadership for the next ten years.

My elevation in local political circles entitled me to rub shoulders with those who could help Basildon from a national level. I attended Labour's 1962 conference of 'Victory for Socialism', a Harold Wilson vehicle, which he dumped once he had become prime minister.

While I was talking to Tom Driberg and Jenny Lee, Harold came up and was introduced by Driberg 'I want you to meet our cloth cap conscience.' Everyone roared out laughing.

I invited Wilson to come to Basildon. He accepted. I liked him from the start, he was able to cultivate people. That was the key to his success.

I was more brusque with people, yet I did not fall into his trap of accepting that the civil service had a right to a point of view. I realised if I played up my aggressive and foul-mouthed don't-give-a-damn image they became frightened and wary of me.

Being a member of the Council also enabled me to see snobbery working at first hand. I recall the time Chris was invited to

Buckingham Palace with me. One day a letter came through the door, Chris said, 'It's from the lord Chancellor'. I didn't believe her 'you silly cow, an invitation to a garden party at Buck House'. I said, 'I'll get publicity by refusing'. Chris said 'No, you're going.'

So there we were, walking through the gates. Chris said to me 'Nice for a boy from Canning Town to walk through this gate, eh, Joe? Especially with me being foreign. Wonder how many there have been like us?' We did not know at that stage that we would be invited back a second time, chauffeur-driven in a civic limousine.

Our garden party was attended by Princess Anne and Prince Philip. When I was presented to the Duke, he asked where I was from, instead of mentioning Basildon I said 'Canning Town, not bad for an East End kid, is it?', he never replied, and moved on quickly. That did not worry me, for I did not like the Duke, as he had never done a real day's work in his life, but was always talking about how people should work hard. This probably coloured how I viewed him when I later wrote to him to complain about the way his awards scheme was being run.

Even so, I was allowed back a year later as Leader of the Council. Poor old Chris, we had no money for a lot of posh dresses, so she wore the same outfit each time, just putting on different shoes.

We stood on the lawn, chatting away, when Chris got pushed and tea went all over her glove. One of the Queen's equerries was responsible. I said ' 'Ere you, 'aven't you got no bloody manners, say sorry when you do something like that.'

'I beg your....'

'Don't bloody well beg pardon, you say sorry you ignorant git!'

'I'm very sorry,' he said.

This time the Queen Mother was there, and she stopped to talk to someone next to Chris and I, but then moved on, much to Chris's disappointment.

I had arrived at Buckingham Palace for a second time because Labour had become a large opposition group, whose battle with the Tories spread, causing meetings to be packed with 100-200 members of the public. These meetings were very charged, and I would play to the crowd. The Tories were scared. With reason.

In 1963, New Town elections were held for the first time in full, so everyone who lived in Basildon could have a say.

The result was overwhelming: Labour 21 seats, Tories three, Rate Payers four, Liberals one. Now things were going to change, there was new wine in the bottles.

Chapter Eight
MOSCOW ON THE THAMES

The 1960s has been much reviled in recent years, but there is no getting away from it, those years were times of social change, they were exciting and alive, a far cry from the miserable world we live in today. There were problems in the world, but people felt they could be solved — and that was not just idealistic fools who thought that way, but realistic men of power. It was in the spirit of the age that I prepared to take control of Basildon New Town. My ten years in charge of the local Labour Party were a whirl of meetings, conferences and social functions. I loved every minute of it. I was fortunate that my employers, Bibby, a firm of building contractors, gave me all the time off work I required. At one stage I was spending more time working for Basildon than for them!

My only regrets looking back are that I was too loyal to certain colleagues, and this cost me and the town dear in the long run. But for a while, I achieved my aim of making Basildon a socialist welfare state with at least pretensions to better things commercially. The people were served properly for the first time.

Our programme for the first term of office had been widely publicised in some detail, but in a nutshell it was the aim of the Labour group to alter the face of local government in Basildon completely.

I had two years to think through the specifics of how we would go about altering the administration and decision making processes. I knew that if we succeeded we would start a transformation of council government throughout Britain. This sounds like a grand claim but I was sure that the old system was ripe for change, and I was confident that the prime minister, Alec Douglas-Home, would soon be replaced by a Labour cabinet which would back us up. And we would need backing up, because I intended to wrest some of the BDC's powers from it, and I knew they and their cronies in Whitehall would put up a fierce fight to jealously guard what they no longer deserved to have: namely the control of Basildon's future.

I knew that many others would be against us when we tried to sweep away such arcane and ineffective institutions as the Clerk of Council, a role which tradition demanded had to be filled by a solicitor. Many old style politicians were going to hate the killing-off of parish-pump politics. We had already been uncompromising in our attitude to the Tories when in opposition, now we were going to continue that policy by having the roles of governing party and opposition officially recognised. They also had a shock coming to them when they discovered that we were not going to allow any of them to serve on council committees.

So I walked in to my new office on the first morning as Leader of the Council. It was a job we had specially created, we had not asked anyone's permission to do it, we just went ahead and invented what was to become the model of all other council's chief political executives. To live up to its expectations, I knew I had to be as uncompromising with my council officers as I was with the Tories.

The heads of the council departments were waiting to see me. They had not come to listen to me spout words of wisdom, they had come to tell me what to do, as they had told previous head councillors what to do. Instead, I started by giving them a brief and broad outline of the Labour group's policy.

They were told that in future, the council was going to raise its house building programme from 20 a year to 500. They were told how all contracting out of council works would be replaced by a Basildon direct labour force. They were told about contracts to sell transport and petrol to the council being scrapped — the council would build its own petrol stations and purchase vehicles directly henceforth. They were told that the council would make provision for these ambitious plans by building large works depots.

The town engineer, Stanley Wadsworth, was the first to speak.

'Oh you can't do that, no, no, no. Now let me tell you, I'm quite prepared to take a few more men on.'

At that, the treasurer, a chap called Cousins, chipped in.

'I wouldn't allow him to have the money for that. I'm responsible for the rates that are collected — not you; I'm the treasurer.'

The only ones who seemed prepared to back me were the housing officer, John Bates, and Ken Cotton, a young architect who was standing in for one of the departmental heads.

I said that was okay, and fair enough. I opened a desk draw and took out some pencils and paper, and then gave them out to everyone who had objected to the policies. When they asked what the pencils and paper were for, I told them quite curtly.

'Your resignations. I only want you to do what I want to do. So will you please write your resignations. The work you gentlemen do is not worth a toss. I can go up the labour exchange and get half a dozen labourers — they'll do your jobs, sitting in your offices, 'cos it's all the people underneath in the pyramid, they're the ones doing all the work. You don't do nothing, so just write your resignations out. I'll give you all a month's notice, so there's no need to stay here — you can go home now. Clear your desks, it's 12 o'clock now, clear them by 2 o'clock, every one of you.'

I wish that I could have taken a photograph of them all just at that moment. They were speechless.

'Out you go, go on!'

They left me alone. Yet as time wore on they returned to the office, furtively, one by one, to come and plead with me. All of them asked me to reconsider, because of course, they assured me, they did not agree with what so and so said, it was all a misunderstanding, I was the leader. So I called them all back again.

'Now gentlemen, who's the boss? Let's remember that and we'll get on well together. I'm the boss man, and you'll do as you're told, 'cos your bosses are out there, they voted for me. So from now on you do as you're bloody well told, or you get out.'

I never had to suffer dissention from another council officer after that.

Next I spoke to the experienced Town Clerk, Alma Hatt, about the idea of replacing his post with that of a town manager, along the lines of the system that existed in the Republic of Ireland. Alma was an advocate of a shake up in the way things were run, although as far back as 1954 he had cautioned against any charges in the local government system with regards to introducing town managers, in an address given to a national conference of urban district council clerks. But he had since re-thought his ideas, as he saw how the stodgy committee system and his own limited role were so ineffective in making and carrying out policy, and powerless to stop the BDC walking all over the council.

I told Alma that whether he was given the new post or not I did not know, he was near retirement age, and I felt it was up to him to show enough commitment to the idea. He replied that he agreed with every word I had to say on the subject of re-structuring, and that he wanted to work with me. He wanted to be the first town manager, but he realised he would not be able to hold the post for long, but he really did want to serve. He went on that I would need him because I would have a terrible job trying to push these plans through.

These plans were later the subject of a BBC2 documentary, and in November 1965, featured in the 'trade magazine' of the councils — *Local Government Chronicle*. As a district of 106,000 with some 70,000 of those living in the New Town, Basildon had reached a size where it could not be ignored.

The article laid out our detailed plan in quite clear and succinct terms. It started off by stating that the old committee system had been removed, and mentioned Alma's ideas in the 1950s.

Ideas were the main feature of the new system: no longer were thoughts going to be held on to in secret, there was to be a free circulation of ideas, in the hope that a freedom of information would stimulate constructive debate, and stop little empires being built.

All sub-committees, with the exception of education, were abolished, to streamline the discussion and decision processes. The committees were to have a maximum of all relevant business put through them, because previously some council matters crept by the discussion stage when they needed to be talked about. To balance this increase in the workload of councillors, more work was delegated to the council officers.

The chairman and vice-chairman of the new committees were to have far more power than previously, giving them the ability to break deadlocks and any stagnancy in the process. They also were given the power to set up panel and study groups to look into specific problems.

The clerk to the council had become the chief executive officer, with responsibility for promotion, direction and co-ordination of the council's programme. His deputy was designated associate clerk, and given chief officer status. His role would now take over all the traditional duties of the old-style town clerk, that is, legal and committee administration work.

The committee chairmen were formed into a policy committee, which would give overall direction to planning, and could consider matters referred to them from another committee. Only the executive committee reported to the council, its nine members submitting new proposals to the council.

Two-member committees had been set up, which operated on a day-to-day basis. Their members came only from the controlling party on the council. For formal meetings, a third member, a 'shadow chairman', was in attendance, but did not have the power to vote.

Advisory groups could be formed as necessary to advise committees on matter where specialist knowledge was needed.

A town manager was to be appointed who would have responsibility for preparing the council's major plans, reviews of new projects and proposals and supervising all departments (although they would not be expected to get involved at professon or technical levels). The town manager would report to the executive committee.

Other innovations included a time limit of 30 minutes for previously submitted questions at the opening of each council meeting, and project papers to be made public to keep the people informed of how their money was being spent.

The overall aim was to release councillors from superfluous detail and reverse the trend that I had noticed in the decline of the calibre of councillors themselves. Broad thinking and encouragement to make decisions effectively were the keys.

The article went on to mention how we had achieved our building figure of 500 houses a year after three years.

I was interviewed for the piece, and explained that not only had the committee changes speeded decision making up, but that we were also able to cut corners, as plans sent to the ministry went off in the knowledge that they would be confirmed by the council.

We also detailed our administration plans for the council departments, which were the result of the work of a study group of seven councillors. These plans were due to be introduced in May, 1966.

I went on to warn other councils, and anyone who read the article that no change would mean the death of local government.

In 1963 our next step was to inform the government of what we were going to do. In the meantime, I had lunch with Harold Wilson, and the result of our discussions were summed up in a letter that he wrote to me a few days later.

'Dear Joe...I give you my word that, on the return of a Labour government, Basildon New Town would be handed over to your council.'

I was overjoyed, and passed the letter around, giving the good news to the local press. Then Labour won the national poll in October 1964. Wilson even attended an election rally with me for Rita Smythe, who unfortunately did not win the Billericay seat for Labour. I wrote to Number Ten, addressing Wilson as 'Dear Harold', and referring him to his promise. A very stilted letter came back from Downing Street. 'Dear Councillor Morgan' it began, no 'Dear Joe' this time.

'You fail to understand that the New Towns were paid for out of tax payer's money, and it would be wrong for them to be handed over to local councils. I have asked the Minister for Housing to meet you to discuss your views on this.'

All of a sudden, I had a strange warped desire to see the Tories back in office — for about 30 seconds, I wondered if Labour would be the same as the Tories — at least up until now I had been able to use them as whipping boys for problems such as the housing shortage. I could hardly blame my own party at national level to everyone in Basildon for this huge setback. The distance and coldness the Tory housing ministry had shown me was being repeated in the tone of my correspondence with the new administration. Had the civil servants got to Wilson and his cabinet so quickly. No wonder Tony Benn was to later bemoan being lectured about the 'realities of power'.

I met with the ministry, but received no joy at all. This was the first time I crossed swords with Dick Crossman in power, as he had been appointed the Local Government and Housing Minister. And present was Jack Diamond, the permanent secretary to the Treasury. He made it abundantly clear that Basildon would never be handed over to the local authority. This is why, years afterwards, I have remained sceptical over the claims of the government that they will now hand the houses in towns over if the council wins enough support in a ballot. Promises do not mean a thing to national politicians, and later on I will explain how the odds have been deliberately stacked against the council ever gaining complete control of its own town.

In the meantime I had to contend with Crossman, and at the newly formed Department of Economic Affairs, George Brown, and his number two, Tony Crosland. More awkward and annoying to deal with than any of these, though, was Dame Evelyn Sharp, who was still the power behind the throne at Local Government and Housing. From his diaries, Dick Crossman seems to have been half in awe of her, and it showed in much of his early decision making.

I went to Alma to see the Dame, and tell her about the changes we were going to make. She utterly rejected the idea and told me to get out.

'Let me tell you Madam, I'm going to operate it and I don't give two monkeys for you. I don't like you as a person, I certainly don't like you as a civil servant, and we are adamant!'

After that I received a summons to travel up to Whitehall again, though this time to see Dick Crossman. He started off by telling me that I could not talk to civil servants the way I had to the Dame.

I replied,

'Dick, these people are here to advise you. You don't have to take their advice if you don't want to. You're elected by the people, and I'm elected by the people. I'll talk to civil servants how I like, and if they don't like it, they can lump it. Or they can talk back to me the same way — I don't mind. But we're having a Town Manager, and that's all there is to it.'

Crossman persisted, and told me he would make it illegal for me to make such changes.

'Then put me and all my group in prison, because we're going to operate it, and you can do what you like. You have too much control over local government, and I'm going to break it.'

He asked me who I thought I was, and really tore me off a strip. All to no avail. I went out and went ahead.

There was uproar in the national press over not appointing any opposition councillors onto the committees. I was accused of being a dictator. Crossman called me back again.

I made a perfectly simple point that he had no answer to. I asked how many Tories there were in the cabinet. Dick said that was different, it was central government.

'I'll tell you what, you put Tory M.P.s in the Labour cabinet, and I'll put Tory councillors on my committees. As soon as you've done that, they can come on. Well, I know you're not going to do it, so no Tory comes on mine — please yourself. Tell Harold he can have the top Tories sitting with him in Downing Street, and I'll have the top Tory sitting with me in Basildon.'

'You think you're the prime minister!' Dick protested.

'I am! I'm the prime minister of Basildon, and don't you forget it.'

I walked out and continued to run Labour-only committees.

I do not claim any great insight into the characters of Wilson and his cabinet, but I think that the few impressions I gained of those I knew shed some light not only on why the civil service were able to manipulate them, but also why I could get so frustrated with my own party's government. The failures of Wilson's government played a large part in the electoral backlash that Basildon's Labour party suffered in the latter half of the 'sixties, which allowed the polytechnocrats and ex-Tories to infiltrate and destroy everything the party of Morgan, Fairer and Elder created.

Harold Wilson had a fantastic memory for people, their faces, their names and what they did. He had the ability to make you feel his only confidant within seconds. He was one of Labour's greatest figures, in that he made labour a party of modern government. His greatest faults were his love of intrigue, and his loyalty to so-called colleagues, who would have sold their mothers to a Shanghai brothel if it meant power for them. They let him down, and allowed the civil service to back him into numerous corners. Today he is denigrated as a con artist, but for all his faults, Labour has had nobody with a fraction of his political ability since.

George Brown was a blustering man, full of his beloved alcohol and his own ego. I never felt at ease in his company, feeling that he gave the impression of someone who would betray socialism at the drop of a hat. On the two or three occasions when we were together, things always denigrated into heated arguments, not helped by the fact that the more he drank, the looser his tongue became. He once told me at a dinner to calm down, and take it easier. I told him that if I calmed down as much as him, I would stay as I was.

He was instrumental in stopping my plans to develop Basildon's industrial base, frightened about pressure from the already dying London docks and their unions. He was not fit to hold a cabinet post, I shudder to think what he was like as Foreign Secretary, but Wilson had to keep his right wing quiet somehow.

Tom Driberg was chairman of the party, and on the national executive, but a major cabinet post eluded him because of his obvious homosexuality. He was as smooth as oil, and I had no time for him, though in fairness he kept to his left wing views whatever. But then he had money, and could afford to be whatever he wanted.

Once I was invited to one of Driberg's gatherings at Bradwell House, his palatial home, which was stocked with plenty of the male Young Socialists who regularly stayed there. He wore his sexuality like a badge, seeming to want to punish himself for the obvious scorn and embarrassment he inspired by calling any man he spoke to 'my dear boy' and his bitchy sarcasm that increased as he drank, which unfortunately was often. Unlike George Brown, though, he was wasted, like him or not, I thought that Driberg had ability, possibly enough to be premier, but he could not come to terms with the responsibilities of public life.

At the Scarborough party conference in 1963 I had a long discussion with him and Nye Bevan's widow, Jennie Lee, about working class representation. I accused them of creating a working class party with no working class representatives. They and other intellectuals had hi-jacked the organisation at the top. With as much mockery as affection he would refer to me as 'our cloth cap conscience'.

On another occasion we had a fierce argument about Spain, with Driberg asking why working class people went to a 'filthy fascist country' for their holidays. I told him it was because they could not afford Cannes or Monte Carlo unlike him and all the other cheque-book socialists.

Another curious aspect of his career was that when he was adopted as M.P. for Maldon, he was not even a party member. His selection had been wangled by the Eastern region agent. Driberg took great delight in boasting of this to those of my outlook, in between salivating over and ogling any young waiter who might be serving at whatever Labour function we were attending.

Bob Mellish was bitter that he was never made Minister of Housing. He was treated badly by Wilson and the intellectuals of the party. He was the one top-flight Labour politician I was at ease with. He came from a similar background to myself, so was able to understand the dreams of ordinary people, yet capable of being brutally frank and straightforward. He did not trust his colleagues, but remained loyal to them throughout his career.

He shared my hopes of re-housing Londoners in good quality homes and decent communities. He and I were working on a scheme to give the London boroughs vast areas of land in Wickford. The Basildon council would have enjoyed 10 per cent of the re-lets indefinitely, thus providing a flow of housing for second and third generation families at no cost to our council. In addition it would probably have provided a built-in Labour majority for

113

years to come. Our scheme never saw fruition after I left the council, and my successors never seemed keen to follow-up what I had started.

Bob Melish, now Lord Melish, then resigned from the Labour Party and accepted a most lucrative position as the chairman of the Docklands Development Corporartion. I was disappointed that he accepted such an offer, as the Corporation seemed intent on destroying traditional working class areas for the sake of 'yuppie' units for the well heeled.

I knew just how fed up he was when he asked me who the new wave in Basildon left wing politics were; 'polytechnocrats and refugees from the Tory and Liberal Parties,' was my answer. He quipped back only half in jest, 'no Joe, I meant Basildon, not the National Executive.'

Tony Greenwood disliked me intensely. From his position in the cabinet he viewed me as uncouth, ignorant and unsuitable. The loathing was mutual — I once told him that I trusted him like Hitler liked bar mitzvahs.

Greenwood was a snob and a careerist.

I wrote to Wilson about Greenwood's attitude towards me, and he replied in defence of him as a cabinet minister, but in no way did the letter rebuke me for my angry tone or accusations. After that, Greenwood refused to speak to me again, and I did not lose any sleep as a result.

How Michael Steward ever became a cabinet minister is still a mystery to me. I have never met a more inept person, he was like a frightened mouse who might flinch at a harsh word. He was a nice, quiet man, totally unsuited to the rough and tumble of Westminster.

I was asked by Transport House's Local Government Officer, Michael Ward, to brief Stewart, then shadow minister for housing, on the scandalous housing and brick shortages for a party political broadcast which was part of Labour's 1964 General Election campaign. Thankfully, Stewart never became the Minister, as he had not a clue about housing, and struggled to grasp even the basics.

After three days coaching and explaining to him what a mess the Tory housing policy was, I did not hold out much hope of a rousing and telling attack by him. The broadcast came across as weak, with Stewart offering a very ineffective argument.

I was interviewed by local news a few days afterwards on the same subject, and I like to feel I did immeasurably better than Stewart. From then on, I was increasingly invited to speak at regional meetings on housing.

I never met Michael Stewart again, but I was as surprised as anyone that he became the Foreign Secretary. I am sure that the Soviets and the C.I.A. must have held celebratory parties. Even in his diaries, Crossman seems to have thought him able, but I shall always remember him as the man I almost had to explain what a brick shortage meant to house building.

Dick Crossman was a complex man who was ill at ease with the majority of the people who made up the Labour Party. He was a donnish figure, who had no idea how these same people lived. He showed disbelief when I told him how Chris, who was on shift work at the time, had to rise at 5am to start work. In his cosy world everyone wore bowler hats and worked from nine to five. Yet he was a passionate socialist in his own manner, having been spurred on by the sights he saw in pre-war Berlin, where like me he met a German girl he would marry.

He was completely dominated by his civil servants, especially Dame Evelyn, who terrified him. I suspect he was also a little bit scared of me, an uncouth East Ender who wielded so much influence with his own M.P.s within the Eastern region.

We had a love-hate relationship down the years, but he would listen to me, rapt by my tales of working class life, which fascinated him. He often invited me to the Commons or his office, and would laugh out loud at my frank pronouncements on political matters. When he complained of how weary he was of making decisions, and all the in-fighting in the party, i told him that there was nothing wrong with the party or the Labour government, just the bastards in it. He roared with hilarity, telling me that I was a scoundrel and a villain, but probably right. We mainly fell out over the influence of what I termed the 'homosexual mafia' — the civil service, he disagreed that they were a cancer in central government, but his laughter at my collective description of them, confirmed what I suspected about their masonic clannishness.

I was able to explain my ideas about 'Moscow on the Thames' to both the press and television, and never felt misrepresented, though it was often a bit dispiriting to see a half hour interview cut down to 20 seconds of air time!

Locally I had the support of two very able reporters, Peter Lucas, who has since gone on to write books about Basildon, and Ken Stone, a reporter on the 'Basildon News'. Both helped to build me up, and although Peter was unbiased, I have to admit that Ken frequently advised me on political tactics, and was a one man 'think tank', responsible for such schemes as warden controlled housing, a new housing points system and Wat Tyler Park, a lasting and beautiful monument to our desire to give something worthwhile to everyone who lived in the area.

I was approached to speak on our new council system up and down the country. I was also considered good copy by the national press, which quickly labelled Basildon 'Moscow on the Thames' — I think it has been applied to several London boroughs since, but I revelled in the attention it brought us, from whatever quarter.

Dan Smith was at the time effectively prime minister of the North. He was trusted by Wilson and the most powerful local government figure in Britain. It was inevitable that we should meet, as Wilson had appointed him to look after the North East, and to head up most of the bodies for economic growth and housing and local government re-organisation. More importantly, he also had the nod on appointments to all Quangos, which were multiplying at a great rate at the time, as they were seen to be the answer to nearly every problem or need for administration.

In 1965 Michael Ward felt that I was beginning to achieve a similar standing in the Eastern region, and Dan Smith had been reading about me, so Transport House arranged for us to meet and discuss ideas.

Alf Dove and I went along to the meeting at a high-class London restaurant. I was impressed by Smith's immense knowledge of the problems facing local councils, allied to his obvious enthusiasm for creating new industry and new development plans.

He was enthusiastic about my re-organisation ideas, and put forward some thoughts on the subject of his own. At the time I was having difficulty in deciding the best way forward over the problem of improving committee efficiency. Smith pointed me in the direction that the Labour group in Basildon eventually took. When I mentioned that I wanted to scrap the post of Town Clerk, he said the best scheme he had seen was the Town Manager idea in Ireland.

His ideas for local administration extended to doing away with all local authorities, and replacing them with regional governments. He saw himself as the leader of the North and Midlands, with me in charge of the East and South East by Illyad Harrington, the G.L.C. boss. I think this was the start of his own desire to set up his own little empire, which eventually led to his downfall. He advised me for some six months on Basildon's re-organisation.

At one stage he told me he wanted all the building agencies formed into a national body, promising me that 'I would get Harold to put you on that'. This was another facet of the man, the giver of posts. He had many sinecures and jobs within his gift, and I think many of them were given in return for financial considerations. But even all his salaries from his numerous posts and the money he accepted in bribes were not enough for him, and eventually his greed led to his part in the Pouslsen corruption case.

He was the jewel in the crown of Labour's local government team, and was genuinely concerned with the welfare people of the

116

depressed North East. It was a waste of talent for him to end up behind bars, where I understand that he ran a legal advice surgery for his fellow inmates. But surely, he wanted above all the money, to be the first leader of a council in Britain, prior to setting off on his quest for a regional prime ministership. But Joe Morgan got there first.

A Consultant Director of Shell's management was another who had noticed what we were doing in Basildon, and he wrote to me saying how interested he was, and could he take me out to lunch?

I ended up having half a dozen such lunches with him, where he advised me on how I should recruit the Town Manager, and just what his brief should be. I agreed that he could sit in on recruitment. He recommended that the Town Manager should not get involved in any of the work expected of the Town Clerk; 'get him to go out — even if you never see him — and concentrate on getting industry into the town and commerce to sell Basildon.'

In the vein of Silkin before him he said that the aim of the enterprise should be to get business people talking about Basildon in the same frame of mind that they would mention Manchester or Birmingham. That way a city would be created, which in turn would lead to a region, just as I had proposed in my plan for a Thames region. He said he had seen that idea, and thought it fantastic; he asked if he could send me some ideas on it of his own: they made provision for an area running from Southend through Basildon to Thurrock. Over the telephone he said 'I don't have to tell you how many Tory voters that makes and how many Labour voters — it would give you control for evermore'. He was right there too. In the 1966 general election Eric Moonman won the local seat for Labour.

I contacted the leaders of the other authorities involved, and gained the support of the majority of them. I submitted a report to Transport House, but George Brown would not even look at the idea. He was too busy with his own little pigeon — a Kent- Essex conurbation, which would have been largely composed of a strong Tory population.

This idea never took off, and went the same way as my plan. George Brown's other consideration was the emphasis in my plan for building a dock at Pitsea Marshes, with a service road to Basildon. This smacked of draining the dying dock industry in London, something that was already a fact due to the development of Tilbury. The difference here was that I would be creating new docking jobs and building housing to accommodate the work force that such a scheme would attract. All George Brown was worried about was the possibility of a dock strike, he could not see beyond the newspaper headlines.

People applied from all over the world for the post, and we spent five days interviewing the candidates. The interviewing team went against my advice and picked David Taylor, then the chief welfare officer of the National Coal Board. They were impressed by the ex-miner who had worked his way to the top. I did not like him from the first, and as events turned out, for all his flamboyance, he was a flop as Town Manager, not being able to take the pace. Those who did not understand his remit thought him wonderful, but if they they had known he was meant to be creating a city instead of improving his golf handicap, they might have seen him with the same eyes that I did.

In fact, prior to Taylor being appointed, we had already given the post to the man who deserved it most, Alma Hatt. He had seen his hopes come to fruition, and was Basildon and Britain's first Town Manager. But fate chose to step in on the very first day of his appointment, and he suffered a heart attack at work. Alma was taken to a London hospital, but did not recover. What a tragedy that a man who had served the town for so long was cut down at the moment of his personal triumph. At least he did not live to see it all descend into the mire. And that all started with David Taylor.

Amid a wealth of publicity, I had been formally made Leader of the Council, yet nothing was heard from Whitehall or Westminster about it. But I knew we had won when Wilson wrote a letter to me, addressed to 'Joe Morgan, Leader of Basildon Council'. Wilson was writing to tell me that he was coming to open the new Ford research plant at Dunton, and he wanted to see me whilst he was in town.

Other councils began to write to me, wanting to know more, so I spent a fair amount of my time addressing Tory and Labour councils regarding the streamlining of local government. On the whole, these ideas were generally accepted, and others began to put them into practice.

Wilson came to open Dunton, and made no direct references to the changes the Labour group had wrought, so I took it that was the nearest to approval we would get from central government. He did not stand on the same platform as me for a while afterwards, but I will relate an amusing incident from when another member of the cabinet took it upon himself to visit our part of Essex.

The tale is purely anecdotal, but it illustrates the sort of snobbery that continued to prevail when I came into contact with those who thought themselves superior to me — in this case, some company directors of the Standard Telephone Co. (STC).

A few months before Wilson came down to open Dunton, STC held a big ceremony to herald the first use of a new transcontinental telephone line. Tony Benn, as Minister of Telecommunications, and yours truly were invited along to the bash. All day the STC bigwigs fawned on him, but were in turn incredibly rude to me, not just ignoring me — which I could have dealt with, but being excessively acid towards me, and more importantly, the office I held.

At the end of the day we moved through to the foyer of their offices, where three paintings were to be handed out to mark the occasion. One was an original, which was to hang in the main entrance in a place of honour, the other two were copies of it for presentation. The STC bigwigs called Tony forward to accept his copy, but he brusquely and rightly advised them that the nature of my office meant I should be presented with a picture first.

I immediately walked over to the original, picked it up and handed it to my chauffeur, telling him to put it in the civic car. Tony gave a broad grin, and quietly said 'well done, that's put them in a whirl'. As I was leaving, a rather embarrassed member of staff who had been appointed to correct my 'error' approached and started to speak.

'Never mind MATE, I'm not fussy, I'll keep the one I've got.'

Ever since it has given me a chuckle each time I look a the painting, as it hangs on the wall of our humble bungalow. At the time of writing this book (1992) I contacted STC to find out the worth of my original. After many calls back to them, I received an answer from someone at head office. In a very frosty tone they told me that they had no trace of where they had purchased the original or the copies from, and it was made clear they would not be finding out.

In my political life I used my friendship with the Catholic Church to garner votes in my ward, which had a sizeable Catholic population, certainly the largest in Basildon. I made a Catholic priest, Father O'Gorman, my civic chaplain. He was also a firm friend and drinking partner. I also cultivated the friendship of the local Knights of Columbia, who were to the Catholic Church what the Masons were to the Tories and the civil service.

Father O'Gorman should have been good for my image if nothing else, but it did not always work out that way. One St Patrick's night we were both in the middle of a serious drinking session. He was wearing my chain of office around his neck and joining in the singing of Rebel songs. Suddenly a woman grabbed the stage microphone and tried to stop the singing. A fight broke out, and quickly escalated. My chaplain came over to me, chain still swinging from his neck, and said 'come on Joe, let's get stuck in!' Before I could stop him, he flew into the midst of the fray.

Yet for all that, He was one of the most lovable and kind men I have known. He would fight tooth and nail to stop any Catholic parishioner being evicted for falling behind in their rent, ringing me up and asking me to personally intervene, delaying any action until he had personally raised the amount that was owed. Basildon lost a great man when he was later transferred to a London parish. Before then we connived to get Government assistance in having a Catholic school built in town.

In 1967 the Church decided to build a part state-owned school in Brentwood. Father O'Gorman asked if there was any way that the school could be built in Basildon instead. I was wary of promising help at first, it was bad enough taking on politicians without upsetting the local bishop as well.

Eventually I agreed to help, seeing that it actually made sense to have the school nearer the larger population centre. I knew that Bob Mellish was a staunch Catholic, and a holder of the Grand Order of the Knights of Columbia. I knew Bob to be keen to be awarded a special knighthood from the Pope. I wrote to him accordingly.

Bob replied to my letter, and contacted a priest who had some sway in the siting of the school, a Canon Hurley. The Canon in turn contacted the Local Education Authority about the matter, but stressed that he only wanted Bob to get involved as a last resort.

As it turned out, Bob referred the matter to Tony Crossland, who was now at Education, and it was Crossland who told the Diocese that the State grants would only fund a school built in Basildon. So it was that St Anselm's was built.

Father O'Gorman was grateful, and at each election continued to remind his flock who it was who looked after its interests.

But it took more than just turning up at church the week before polling day to enjoy the size of personal vote that I received time after time. I made promises and kept them. Basildon enjoyed meals on wheels, bus passes, greater freedom for tenants, more efficient repairs and even a convalescence home on the South Coast. Tenants liaison was created, they were allowed a voice and a vote on the council housing committee. Council works shop stewards were allowed a say at council meetings as well. We were not a faceless bureaucracy.

Democracy and fairness was practised, not just preached. All council staff salaries were given London weighting, and I specifically asked them all to work for loyalty and a socialist cause. This may sound pie in the sky, but it gave them a sense of purpose.

I continued my practice of the Sunday morning walk that had started in Barstable ward by going around with other councillors — 'the red guard' the press dubbed them — and asking people what their problems and complaints were. Every Sunday I would walk through the housing areas of Basildon with my notebook. Even if it was only a cracked paving stone that either had not been reported or neglected it went in the book. If the problem had been neglected,

I would find the officer responsible on the Monday morning and discipline them for losing that sense of power I was trying to instil.

One of the best publicised of such cases was that of the dip in the road. In the early 'seventies, after heavy rains, this particular irregularity in the tarmac looked like a village pond. People were always being soaked by passing traffic as a result. A chap complained to me about this state of affairs.

I took the local press along with me, filled the dip with water from a hose, and stood by the edge of it with a fishing line, for the benefit of the photographer. Then I gave them their quote. 'Look, we pay our engineer £12 thousand a year, and he's not worth 12p unless he gets this filled in by Monday morning.'

The hole was duly filled. However unfair this tactic seems, it got things done. People began to say that if anything needed to be done, Joe Morgan would ensure it was done.

Housing was our biggest challenge, the council waiting list stood at 1,000 names when the Labour group came to power, and we cleared it within three years. We did this by raising the civic building programme to the promised rate of 500 a year, and I demanded housing from the BDC, with varying degrees of success. It then became our priority to house people as quickly as possible, second generation New Towners receiving their new keys in a week. I also fought for, and obtained from the War Department, the right for Army leavers to be granted housing in the New Towns.

The main thorn in the side of our housing programme was that as a council, we only controlled a small percentage of available houses. The BDC still controlled the vast majority of houses in the town, and were unwilling to talk to anyone from the council most of the time. The board still did not have a single member of the council on it, from either Labour or Tory. All the political parties in Basildon agreed that the BDC and their board were high-handed in all dealings with anyone from outside their headquarters at Gifford House, unless they came from Whitehall, home of their masters. The situation had worsened when Labour came to power, and we only saw the board once throughout the whole of 1964. The events of that meeting sparked off a huge three-way row between the council, the BDC and the Minstry in the shape of Dick Crossman and Dame Evelyn Sharp....

Chapter Nine

CROSSMAN AND THE
GIFFORD HOUSE GANGSTERS

Before that fateful meeting with the Board of the BDC, I had continued my campaign in the Council chamber and the press against what I saw as the self-interest and arrogance of the Corporation, which led to inefficiency and downright scandalous housing conditions.

The BDC, led by Charles Boniface, was churning out sub-standard housing that had been ill-conceived in respect of estate layout and housing densities. Parts of Basildon were already on their way to becoming slums through the pig-headedness of Boniface and his minions.

One housing estate in particular, Ghyllgrove, had been turned into what I termed in the local press 'a little Stepney': houses were crammed onto the available land at a high density figure of 15 to the acre; the layout was soulless and soul-destroying. What was worse, these houses were only a few years old and already were showing serious construction defects.

At the Council we had refused a planning request from the Corporation to build 50 house in Luncies Road at a density of 17 to the acre. This argument hit the national press. Denial of planning permission was the only weapon we had against the Whitehall backed might of the BDC. Yet they were still contemplating redeveloping Laindon at a density of 20 to the acre. We were not going to allow Basildon to become a concrete jungle, and end up like other pushed together estates up and down the country.

Examples of Corporation houses falling apart began to feature more and more in the local papers. Houses only 18 months old were visibly cracking badly indoors. The tenants could hear their homes being torn apart at night.

Such a case concerned the Labegueries, who lived on the Sunnedon estate in Vange. Local Councillor Mick Crew and myself took up their case with the BDC. It took the Corporation six weeks to fill cracks in that were wide enough to drive a pencil into. We had to contact the Corporation no less than six times to get them to taken any action. Their response was, 'don't worry, the roof won't fall in.' The same way as they had not fallen in on the Bardfield houses. But that was because the walls fell down first.

I publicly attributed the standard of Corporation housing to bad workmanship and a lack of control at the time of their construction. The BDC was given carte blanche to flout building standards by the Government, and could let houses without them being inspected. One of Wilson's election promises was that he would provide more building inspectors to combat the headlong rush to put up as many houses as cheaply as possible as quickly as possible, and blow the standards.

The Corporation continued to give excuses. On another estate, the houses had been made by means of a new process, and were known as 'Siprex' houses. They showed bad signs of wear, and I was later able to prove that the process and materials used were faulty. But there was no excuse at Vange, where the houses were built in the traditional way, out of bricks and mortar.

The Cabinet and Whitehall backed the BDC in their housing methods. Industrialised building, the umbrella name given to a whole range of quick building methods, was thought to be the way ahead. But these methods were continually shown to be inadequate. If they did not start to crack and move, then they went the way of the development at Stagden Cross, which became mildewed and damp. They were inadequately heated, having only feeble 'background' radiators installed. This was one case where the press, in this case the Basildon, Billericay and Wickford Standard, was able to embarrass the BDC into doing something. They had run a story on Stagden Cross, and in the following week's issue were able to report how the Health Inspector had been called in on the Saturday, myself and the council on the Sunday, and Galloway and Dant on the Monday, who sound like a double act, and were in fact comedians, namely the Chief Architect and Housing Manager of the BDC respectively. They started to make changes and repairs when they saw their own miserable efforts close up.

Dick Crossman and his number two, Bob Mellish, both agreed with industrialised housing, but then, they did not have to live in them. Neither did they have to live on 'open plan' estates, drawn up by people who lived in large houses with large gardens and big fences and conifers for privacy round the outside.

'Rational' housing was the euphemistic name given to industrialised building, and we did use some of the methods it offered in our council house construction programme. Many of our houses were 'Rat-trad', a mixture of modern methods for quickness and traditional bricks for sturdiness. They were cheaper than entirely brick houses, stronger and better made than the BDC's industrialised efforts and nearly as cheap.

It was not just housing where the arrogance of Gifford House ridiculed the whole concept of local government, as I first clashed with Charles Boniface over the siting of the town's college of further education. The County Council, the Urban Council and the BDC had a long discussion about this matter, and came to an agreement on where the college was to be built.

Then Boniface turned round and said the Corporation was not prepared to convey the land. This is what I meant by my phrase of 'faceless dictators' that I later used in the press. The Council and the people of Basildon were being held to ransom by the Gifford House gangsters.

What really irritated me and compounded the problem no end was that frequently both our Council and the County Council had to carry out idiotic directives from the BDC, and we ended up carrying the can when Crossman or any other Minister involved found out about it. We were deemed responsible for the money being wasted, even though we were doing what we had to do by law under the New Towns Act.

To even try and contact the BDC was a major effort in itself. As a fellow Councillor called Curtis put it at the time, 'they've surrounded themselves…with an army of young ladies…who either haven't a clue, or who tell you that who you want is in consultation'.

We finally fell out with the BDC in a big way over two issues; lack of provision for garages and children's play areas. Neither of these might seem earth shatteringly important, but the consequences of not building garages on the estates and setting aside safe areas for children to enjoy were an ever faster descent into ghetto-like lives for the families who lived in these areas. Cars would be parked on roads and verges, where they would be eyesores, a hazard to moving traffic and an open invitation to thievery and vandalism.

It was not even accepted that working class people would need garages, as the Corporation failed to notice the increasing affluence of particularly the young, and a desire to own cars. I put myself in the shoes of the young, and I knew they would all want cars the minute they got their first wage packet, because I certainly would have done. This mistake cost the tax payer a small fortune, for the BDC was funded out of central Government. They have had to widen roads and build off-road parking, far from ideal.

Without their own playgrounds the children would be forced to play in the road, with the obvious consequences that would lead to. As they grew older, they would be tempted to roam the streets in little gangs, and that was the start of the slippery slope called urban decay that London was already experiencing at the time. One Board member clearly showed how out of touch he and the others were with the real world, when he opined that perhaps children wanted to play in the steet. Perhaps babies want to eat broken glass, but would you let them?

Unless the Council had representation on the board of the BDC, we were never going to make any headway with our policies. Already, our struggles with the Corporation had gained us some popularity, but at by-elections people associated us with the struggling national Labour Government and did not know how else to register their frustration with the BDC. Inevitably we started to lose ground to the Tories, through no fault of our own, and at a time when the Labour Group were the only set of people who had been changing things and who could, given a chance, still bring about a better deal.

We resolved to go to Crossman and demand better representation. When I wrote to Wilson, he just palmed me off, saying it was the Government's intent to broaden representation, but he did not detail what he was going to do, or when he intended to do it.

Alf Dove and I had an appointment with Crossman on 12th January, 1965, confident that we had the backing of all the political parties in Basildon and every citizen of the town.

For an hour and a half we furiously argued with Crossman and Dame Evelyn Sharp. At one stage I banged the table so hard I broke a cigarette lighter. We were demanding not just democratic representation on the board, but the handing over of the Corporation's house and factories.

All this was a complete anathema to Dame Evelyn, and she was dead set against the slightest concession. She tut-tutted me at one stage, and I was not in a mood to be condescended to by someone who had turned a blind eye to my accusations of corruption, and was intent on making 100 thousand people's lives a misery for the sake of her own ego.

'You shut your mouth', I shouted at her — she was visibly shaken.

Dick Crossman recalls in his diary that for that day how he had seen Harlow UDC before our deputation, he remarked on how nice they had been. We must have come as something of a rude awakening.

We were already in the bad books before we even set foot in his office. Both he and the Dame had been angered by the newspaper reports of our attacks on the Corporation. We were told that neither of us would ever be put on the Board of the BDC. Crossman talked down to us, and even tried to lecture us on the meaning of socialism! I put him straight too.

'You learned your socialism from books; I learned mine from the East End.'

We left in high dudgeon, but a fortnight later, one of our councillors, Cyril Thirkettle, was nominated and put on the board, rather than a lady who had originally been named. It was only one voice, it was a compromise, but it was a start.

Crossman was later to admit that the Dame (she was later made a Lady for her efforts) was over protective of the various development corporations, but he never dared say as much in her presence.

Crossman fell out with me again not too long afterwards. He came to Basildon to speak at an election rally. I refused to share the platform with him, which gave the press another field day. My reasons were twofold: not only had he just increased the rents in New Towns, he had refused to take any action against the corporation after I had advised him of alleged corruption in their handling of contracts. His reasoning was that if an investigation did prove that corruption existed, it would embarrass the Government. If he was worried about the election, I would not have minded waiting a few weeks to nail the crooks. I do not think that was his major consideration though. Whitehall had got their own way again.

I accused Crossman of bowing down to what I saw as a body of people with selfish and ultimately evil intent. Everywhere I looked, I could see the almost Masonic hold they had on various Ministers and M.P.s. This was no paranoia, just self evident fact. I told Crossman he was an intellectual scab, and that he was terrified of the Civil Service.

From the look on his face, I thought Crossman was going to explode. He ordered me out of his office, and told me I would not be welcome again until he got an apology. I looked him full in the face.

'God, is this what we worked our guts out for, to get elected a lackey of the Civil Service?'

I did not expect an answer. Over my shoulder I added, 'if you think I'm letting go of this scandal then you don't know me.'

So there we sat, me in the audience, him on the platform. He was in town four hours, and not once did we speak to each other.

Four months later Crossman's office telephoned mine, requesting that I meet with Bob Mellish. He had now been given special responsibility for the New Towns. This was the first time I got to know Bob, and we hit it off straightaway.

Bob told me that the present Chairman of the New Town wished to retire for personal reasons, and a new man was being appointed. The real reason was not forthcoming, but I knew that behind the scenes the Chairman had been told in no uncertain terms he was ultimately responsible for the fiddling of the contracts, and that he should examine his position. A broad smile spread over my face as I realised that I had won. It became even broader when it was explained that the new chairman was going to have to work in harmony with me.

Another three months passed, then Crossman invited me down to London to discuss the setting up of a liaison committee between the Council and the BDC. I would represent the Council.

I had no embarrassment on meeting Crossman again, I had been right in all that I had said. He shook me warmly by the hand, acting as though nothing had happened. He only made one reference to our previous meeting.

'Oh by the way Joe, I'm replacing the present New Town Chairman.'

'I know, well done.'

I never saw Crossman after that meeting, he left the Government and went back to his first love, journalism. He died not long afterwards. When his diaries were published years later, the press contacted me, asking for my comments. Crossman had made records of all our meetings, but in the published diaries they were heavily edited. He was quite complimentary, even going so far as to say that his civil servants were autocratic and very unfair to local councils.

He ended that chapter with a little character sketch of me.

'A tremendous old villain, a real knockabout demagogue who thundered and bellowed and terrified his own members and anyone who defied him.'

Whether this was affectionate or a dig is difficult to tell, but quite where Dick Crossman got this view of a gentle, mealy- mouthed soul like myself I cannot imagine.

Perhaps it came from those times we spent talking, as he tried to probe what made me tick, what lay behind the passion, the shouting and the stories of East End life. He once admitted to me that he would never understand Joe Morgan.

'You're always trying to fathom me out Dick, aren't you? You know why you'll never understand me?'

I pointed to my head. I knew I was talking to a university-educated Cabinet Minister. ' 'Cos I've got more here than you'll ever have; you know why Dick? You may have been a don at Oxford University, but I've got street training, I was brought up on the streets and I'm street-wise; you never will be. Whilst you're not street-wise you haven't got a hope in hell against me, and neither have the other people like you. I can always beat you.'

One of our last conversations took the following form.

'Joe, do you know what, I believe if you'd been born with all that you have now but in a different environment, you could have been a great figure in this country.'

'But I wouldn't've wanted to have been, Dick. And you don't understand that, do you? I could've been the first M.P. for Basildon, but I didn't want to be. I wanted to be a councillor in Basildon, amongst my people.'

'Why didn't you want to be an M.P. then?'

'You must be joking.'

I pointed to some members beyond the House of Commons bar.

'That lot you've got out there, Labour M.P.s, not one of them is worth that.'

I'll leave you to guess the gesture I made.

'They all have to do as they're told; but in Basildon I'm Number One. They're just a lump of dirt, the whip says to them "behave yourselves, don't vote here, don't vote there". They sit up 'til 2 or 3 in the morning for that? That's not for me: I'm with my wife, happily married with a family in Basildon — whatever I say in Basildon goes.'

Crossman laughed.

'You are a rogue, that's what you are, a villain and a rogue.'

I then regaled him with more tales of ordinary peoples lives, he would listen, fascinated with a class of people who might as well have been foreign, for all he knew about them. He could not accept that people would wait to be paid on a Thursday or Friday so that they could buy a bit of fish and chips, as they had not eaten for a whole day previously. He was incredulous. 'Not in England?'

As we parted for the last time, he told me that he was going down to Kent for a few days for some peace and quiet, 'away from the Morgans of our beloved Party.'

'You need to go further than Kent, Dick, to forget me; I'm your working class conscience that now and again pricks our beloved leaders.'

So off he went, probably glad to get away from me. Leaving me to think back to my times down in Kent, in those far off days of hop picking.

Goodbye, Dick, you were too nice and gentle for politics.

Reviewing Crossman's thought that I could have been a signifi- cant figure at national level had my background been different, led me to wonder what he would have been like if he had come from the East End. I think he would have been a rebel as his early works as a Don show that he wondered if parliamentary democracy was a sham.

The liaison committees never really worked, and our battles over the future of Basildon continued unabated. When it came to

128

industry, the Corporation only concentrated on light industry, such as clothing manufacturers. It is a wonder they let the likes of Ford into the town. I wanted them to concentrate on attracting industry, but they were half-hearted in their efforts. At one stage we thought nearby Foulness would become London's third airport, and I really wanted to have Basildon geared up to reap the results. The BDC never seemed too interested, so it is just as well that the airport ended up at Stanstead.

Whilst they were shy at providing funding and energy for the basic requirements of the town, the Corporation were only too quick and eager to waste money on their own peripheral pet projects. Two of these schemes in particular attracted a lot of debate: a proposed cable television service and a golf course.

Cable television in itself was a good idea; entertainment for everyone employing the very latest technology to keep ugly aerials and relay masts off the streets of Basildon. The BDC went ahead without consulting anyone else and contracted Rediffusion to install the system. The Board of the Corporation then turned around and announced that to fund the scheme there would have to be a levy on the rents of 1/- (5p) a week. This may sound like a trifling sum nowadays, but at the time it was a substantial amount to ask of people already struggling to pay relatively high rents on countryside wage levels. People mumbled and muttered, already having blamed the council for previous rent increases brought about by the cavalier policies of the BDC.

More important, how was the installation of the scheme being funded in the first place? There was an Amenities Fund available to the BDC, so why were they misusing rents? I was prepared to refuse them permission to dig up the roads to lay cables. Yet the Ministry of Housing, with the Minister's consent, refused to intervene. In my opinion their previous appointment of a Rediffusion board member onto the BDC's own board was somehow connected with their hand-washing.

So, eventually cable television was installed in Basildon and everyone had to take it, like it or lump it. At least my interference meant that the charges for cable were not included in the rents. As it turned out, the service is very good, but the principle is that this was not tendered for and was allocated without consultation.

The Basildon golf course involved a protracted and bitter row between one of the Corporation's own Board members, that old strike-breaker, Sir Richard Bonallack (also President of Basildon Golf Society and father to Michael, Captain of the Society and English Amateur Stroke-play Champion) and yours truly.

The BDC applied to the Treasury for money to build a course, and rumours were rife that once built, the facility would be given to a private concern. Subsequently the Board seemed ready to grant the lease of the course to the Golf Society. They were not supposed to do any such thing, and bearing in mind Sir Richard's self interest, I accused the BDC of double-dealing. I threatened to get Crossman to look into the whole question of the golf course. I was blowed if an elitist bunch were going to rob everyone else in the town of the right to recreation.

What really set me dead against anyone remotely connected with the BDC having control of the course was less personal malice, and more to do with what a particular doctor said to me at a social function at the time the row blew up.

'You don't want to argue about this gold course Joe. People will be able to use it — but not everyone....

'What do you mean, not everyone?'

'Well, you know, Jews and blacks.'

'Do you know what you've just done? You've ensured that course becomes a municipal one.'

At the second annual dinner of the Basildon District Golf Society in December 1964, those present were told that a 27 hole course at Kingswood had been given Treasury approval on the condition that it was self-supporting. One of my Labour colleagues, Bert Saunders, the Council Chairman, was at the dinner, when he heard Sir Richard imply that the course would not pass to the Council's control, he suggested in his speech that the course would be a municipal one, and that 'some satisfactory arrangements will no doubt be made to enable your club to play'. This was the start of grave upset. Bonilack implied that if we wanted a golf course we would have to build our own.

For all Sir Richard's carping, it was the decision of the Minister itself to hand the golf course over to the Council. The Board were also stung by remarks that they could not find money for children's play areas, but they could for Board members' golf courses, so they did not dare question the decision or plead their own case.

Yet the Tory Group leader, Harry Withington, gave the Parks Chairman, Bill Archibald, a hard time with a string of questions about the course. Arguments raged about whether it was proper use of a valuable open space close to the town centre.

I got my way, and the course was completed and handed over to the Council. I wanted a grand opening ceremony and an open invitation for the people of the town to attend, but the BDC out-manoeuvred me on that one, and sent the lease through the post in a tacky little envelope.

Another waste of public money was the Basildon Arts Centre. I do not wish to sound like a caricature cockney philistine, but the whole thing was an elitist incidental, and was used for political ends by the Tories. I wanted a permanent arts centre built as part of a Town Hall. Those opposing me were for a temporary arts centre. As this would have to be demolished in a short time it was bound to cost the ratepayers a large sum of money, but they still had their way.

We eventually lost overall control of the council to the Tories, and part of their success was on the back of the Arts Centre. If the centre had put on shows and performances that people would have gone along to watch in enough numbers to make it pay at least part of its way, it would not have been too bad.

Yet I was able to release 'confidential' figures to the newspapers that showed it had made a substantial loss, part of which involved money guarantees given by the council. I reckoned that the centre was going to cost £4,000 a year to subsidise. The Tories always complain about Labour subsidising public services, yet here they were prepared to support plays no-one was turning up to see.

More disturbing still had been the recent elections, when officials from the arts centre had assisted the Tory candidate in my Barstable ward, where newsletters from him were singing the praises of the centre.

I urged the centre to come down out of cloud cuckoo land and put on shows that people wanted to see. I was not only opposed in this view by the Tories, but by some of my own councillors as well. Bill Archibald, egged on by Gerald Krejzl, argued that success was not measured in financial terms alone. I know Bill was involved with the arts centre, and therefore had an axe to grind, but subsequent events proved me right, as the place became an albatross. I was not entirely blind to the need for art as a public recreation. I had asked for free art lessons at the centre, this was criticised as hypocrisy, but it would have cost a damn sight less than the amount of the play guarantees being doled out.

Opposition over other matter than the arts centre began to arise at the time. I respected Bill and Gerald for their point of view, but those who opposed me afterwards had very different motives.

As we lost ground to the Tories, people seemed unable to distinguish between us, the failures of the Wilson government, and the stupid directives of the BDC, there was a sudden influx into the party from 1967-8.

Many of those new members fell into three groups, teachers, ex-Tory Party members and ex-Liberals. I was opposed to people from other parties joining, but I was overruled. I was suspicious of their reasons, and saw them as careerists who could not get what they wanted elsewhere. The teacher element resented the working class members of the Party, and made little attempt to disguise their contempt for what they saw as the people who gave Labour an out-dated 'trouble at mill' image. Image was the word, they were part of the new polytechnic inspired world that Wilson had created, but could not control. They were convinced that by attracting the vote of the professional classes, everything would be rosy.

John Potter was an ex-Tory Party member; an ambitious man who grabbed the opportunity along with a Salvation Army member called Tinworth, to eventually gain election to the party hierarchy as Leader and deputy.

I suspect that Potter would have joined the Monster Raving Loony Party if he felt the call for leadership.

He had wanted to join the Council for quite a while, but I was successful in keeping him out at first. He was only adopted while my back was turned, as I was in Sweden on a fact-finding mission, in an attempt to prove that the BDC were wrong over industrialised housing. That is the problem in the Labour Party, you always have two battles to fight at the same time, and I could not cover my back.

In Sweden I went to see some houses built using the 'Siprex' material. The method had been banned there after a lorry ran into the corner of a block of flats made of the stuff, bringing down the whole building, which fortunately was empty. This would not have happened if the same accident had occurred to a traditional type house. Basildon Corporation made the mistake of building a dozen 'Siprex' houses, and I wanted to prove to the council and the BDC just how dangerous these buildings were. I remember taking an ordinary screwdriver and being able to push it right through one of the walls of these dangerous houses back in Basildon. Everyone had told me I was wrong, and that they were safe, from the BDC to Jim Callaghan for the Government. The 'Siprex' developments are now costing £28 million to pull down in Basildon.

I arrived back home to report my findings to Transport House, only to find Potter waiting for a vacant seat to contest on the Council. He soon got it.

I carried on attacking the BDC, and trying to organise my plans for Basildon as a regional centre. I wrote to Harold Wilson about BDC board representation again in 1967, he again palmed me off by saying that I should talk to Crossman, and that appointments made under his Government had done much to redress the imbalance on the Board. Yet the BDC continued to act in an arrogant manner. Boniface continued to ignore my requests, and acted like a British Empire official talking to some poor native. Yet this man had wanted to become Basildon's Town Manager. I suppose he could not have been any worse than David Taylor, but he never did fill the post, and ended his Corporation days in the 1970s, with little recognition from anyone for his work. That suited me, but might have been a bit harsh on him.

He and his crew were less than pleased when I first dubbed them the 'Gifford House gangsters' when they announced a celebration party for the 21st birthday of the New Town, and I pointed out to the press that the champagne money would have been more wisely spent going towards keeping the level of the previous week's rent rise down. Another rise had been promised for the following October.

I was also running out of patience with Bob Mellish at the time. Although we got on well, he like all other M.P.s came under the influence of civil servants, much to my annoyance. He was not being very helpful in plans I had submitted to him for sites to be used in building London overspill housing. He was trying to wash his hands of the matter, and pass the buck to the Essex County Council.

He did not see eye to eye with me over a regional authority either. He was of the view that large authorities did not work very well, and cited those in London as examples.

On a lighter hearted note, I made a brief appearance in the national press in 1969, when I reported a fish and chip shop for overcharging. The papers carried the story of how I had reported Seafare Restaurants Ltd to Barbara Castle, the Minister for Employment and Productivity.

They had started selling crinkle cut chips instead of straight ones at their shops in Basildon. For the pleasure of the crinkles you were obliged to stump up an extra 2d (1p). Since fish and chips was still the staple diet of many people in town, I soon received complaints about the rise from 9d to 11d a portion. In 1969 this made them expensive chips. The shop claimed that the crinkle cuts were better quality, and were only on a three month trial.

I wanted the Tories to have their chips, and announced our plans for our second term of office, in a booklet entitled 'The way ahead'. It brought a heap of criticism from both the Tories within and without the Party.

I proposed to make more provision for the housing of future generations, namely the third and fourth in town, who were still at school at that stage. I was ridiculed for looking that far in front, but I pointed out how I had also been attacked in the past for the amounts I had spent on the elderly, but everyone in the Council would some day be old, and by making enough provision for the citizens of tomorrow, we would ensure that our dotage was spent in a prosperous lively town, not a dying one.

I also made a strong case for crêches in industry, and also kept on about the need to build garages and widen roads to accommodate the ever increasing traffic burden. I had seen how effective The Lanes in Brighton were, and I wanted a similar mid-town development to encourage people to meet up and give heart and life to what was otherwise just another shopping centre. I wanted features like this to open at night. These were all the sort of things that would help to confer city and regional centre status on Basildon.

Potter and his cronies pooh-poohed these ideas, not because they disagreed with them, but to maximise any embarrassment they could cause me. I ignored them and continued working on the regional plans, and they took full advantage whilst I was so engrossed.

I wonder quite who was behind the attempt to embarrass me further at the local elections, when an ex-carnival queen was chosen as the Tory candidate to stand against me. 'Beauty and the Beast' were the national headlines over articles about the election, which would show her in a glamorous costume and an unflattering photo or caricature of me.

The local Tories were boosted by 500 helpers who came in nationally to help. They really thought that they could dislodge the man who had given the people of Barstable good service with a blonde who could smile nicely for the cameras. I was so much seen as a symbol of local Labour Government policy that they were falling over themselves to beat me.

The day of the poll came, and as all the candidates for the ward stood amidst the vote counting, the Tory glamour queen saw some bundles of votes for her beside a few spoiled ballot papers. She took the spoiled papers to be votes for me, and started shouting 'I've won, I've won'. There was an uproar, and cameras started flashing. Then the Returning Officer announced the result of the 60% turn-out poll. Beauty, 1,900 votes, the Beast, over 5,000.

The crowd went berserk. The queen, her crown snatched away from her, burst into tears, and mascara streamed down her face. I turned to one of the reporters.

'If you're a proper journalist take a photograph of her now, they can stick the queen 'cos I'm the king!'

I had similar success when the Labour Group got back into power, thanks to our plans and my share of the Catholic vote, although we did not enjoy overall control. We had cheerleaders and all sorts of razzmatazz going on. Yet as an interview I gave at the time points out, because I was expecting to be confirmed as Chairman of the Council for the year, I had tried to carry myself with a bit of decorum, since the Chairman was supposed to be above party politics.

I had served on every committee in the chamber, and felt my experience would be enough to stop Potter and the others getting any farther forward with their avowed plan to rid the Party of its 'cloth cap' element.

On a wider scale, I now had a Tory Government to deal with at national level. Yet I got more out of the Tory ministry than I did from Crossman, probably because the Tories did not have to worry about how things looked for their Party, whereas Crossman always had to consider Party image and harmony. And I suspect the Tories were a little frightened of us as well.

I had moved from Barstable to a house in Pinmill during the 'sixties, as our family grew up. I requested to be moved at one stage, and I was given a new house at West Thorpe by the BDC, still my Landlord. People were suspicious that I had used my council position to enable me to be allocated the house, and some even turned up on my doorstep to shout insults. They were wrong, and if they had known me better, they would have realised that I was the last person who would take anything from the BDC. I comforted myself that perhaps they were all Tory agitators from over at Billericay.

Basildon did not become a separate parliamentary seat until 1979, and we came under the Billericay umbrella up until that time. This did cause some resentment to exist between the two areas, but it was only a reflection of a social and political split that had existed for some while.

After Sir Bernard Braine departed from Basildon politics as a result of boundary changes in Essex, Richard Boddy was our Tory M.P., and he did his damnedest to deliberately split the people of Basildon from those at Billericay and Wickford. I had been told by a fellow Councillor that I would be lynched from the nearest tree if I ever set foot in either place, as they were a bedrock of Tory support. In 1964 Boddy was replaced by Edward Gardner, and strangely enough we had quite a good relationship. Like other Essex Tories, he eventually moved on to a safer seat. Basildon and Billericay were finally made separate seats in 1979.

Gardner specifically attacked the Labour Council for making a priority out of housing works for the Laindon, Pitsea and Langdon Hills areas. They were mainly Labour areas, and he claimed (falsely) we were just looking after our own. The happened to be the areas that required priority, but he made it a party political issue. We were able to point out in turn that Billericay and Wickford only contributed 29% of the total New Town rates, but had received 87%

of the private street works money. But by arguing we were falling into his trap.

So faced with attempts inside and outside the party to divide and rule, I prepared to take Potter, Tinworth and their cronies on. I was no longer the building worker with cloth cap they despised so much, in fact I had got myself an insurance round in South Ockendon, a good Labour area, of course. That meant wearing a suit most of the day. What more could they ask from Joe Morgan? I was soon to find out, as I underestimated their cunning and the depths they would sink to for personal aggrandisement.

Chapter Ten
EVERY MAN HAS HIS PRICE

I have often wondered just how much money someone would have needed to offer Joe Morgan for him to do their bidding. I have never taken a bribe, but I have seen plenty of others on the take around in my time with the council. I never forgot Lofty Cousin's little lecture about the canteen forks, and it served me well, but quite apart from using the knowledge that in power, someone, somewhere is always grafting and cheating, I was determined on an ethical level to defeat the backhander boys wherever they were; sometimes this meant turning on people who called you 'comrade', but to me, socialism could only work if those who carried it out were above reproach. No wonder so many of my own side hated my guts. I only ever once turned a blind eye to cheating, and that was the biggest mistake I ever made. But worse than all the graft was the political skulduggery and back-stabbing by the so-called comrades; class distinction was rife in the party.

Potter was not to be trusted, but Eric Batchelor was far worse; I think that he was without scruples.

My first run-in with Batchelor came when the constituency Labour Party voted for a president. One of those in the running was a chap called Bob Chaplin, in many ways a good councillor, but also an embarrassment to the rest of the party because of his self-presentation and domestic life.

Bob would stand up in the council chamber to speak on a subject, but whatever it was would often be forgotten as councillors on all sides looked on incredulously at the unwashed, dishevelled figure before them, his trouser flies permanently at half-mast. You would have thought that his wife would not allow him to go out in public looking like that, at least, until you met her, one of the scruffiest and most loud-mouthed women it has been my misfortune to meet. When I went round to the Chaplin household it was in such a filthy state that it was all I could do to stop myself from vomiting on the spot. Just to top matters off, Bob's children were constantly in trouble with the law, and he would vigorously try to defend them, which was understandable but often less than wise. Yet for all of this, he carried out his duties as a councillor pretty well, certainly far better than most who have followed since.

The votes were cast, and the results were 32 votes for Bob, and 18 for the other candidate, a teacher called Bill Chalk. There was a delay in announcing the result of the ballot, and in fact the result was never read out, at least not in the form that I have just described.

People were getting restless, wondering why they had not heard the result. I looked over to where Batchelor and a few others, were talking. I caught Batchelor's eye and he beckoned me over.

'What's the matter?'

They came right out with it, saying that Bob Chaplin had won the vote, but could not possibly be allowed to become president of the party. It was coming up towards election year, and his image would sit ill at ease with that of the man who represented us when meeting national politicians, other civic figure and chairing meetings. He was a liability. But he had won, fair and square.

'Well what are his results?' I asked.

They showed me the figures on the table. He had won easily. By this time everyone in the room was getting uneasy, some were coming over to see what the delay was. Voices were being raised above the general hubbub that had broken out.

'Well, if he's won it, he's won it,' I argued with irrefutable logic.

'What would you do if we gave the decision the other way around, reversed it?' asked Batchelor.

'You must be joking. You must be joking.'

The others pleaded with me to agree to rigging the vote, 'for the sake of the party', as they put it.

I agreed.

I have regretted that decision ever since. I should have refused, that would of been the end of Batchelor, I could have reported him to Transport House then and there. If I had, I am sure that the Basildon Labour Party would not have started out on the slippery slope that it was later to end up on. Potter and Tingworth might never have come to power. But all I said was 'I won't say anything, but keep me out of it'.

So the result was given as Chalk 32, Chaplin 18. Bill Chalk was totally unaware of the shenanigans that had made him president. Bob Chaplin looked totally shocked, he was sure that he was going to win. I could not look him in the face. I knew I had done wrong, and I was very uneasy about it. But if I thought Batchelor would be happy at that, I was mistaken. But that would come later, in the meantime the party good had been put first, but at the expense of honesty and democracy.

It was always the party first. Everything else was sacrificed to the party good. It was also a justification for everything that the three wise monkeys — Batchelor, Potter and Tinworth ever did. What has passed since those days certainly does not seem to have done the party much good at all. But sometimes this 'party good' policy did not damage an individual's or group's integrity, and in one case, I was able to set the record straight after the party good had been served.

One of the best and most enduring ideas that Cyril Thirkettle had whilst in office was that of a central kitchen for the elderly with an area for leisure activities, somewhere that the senior members of Basildon's community could enjoy socialising, much in the same way that I wanted the centre of town to be a place to encourage young people to meet.

In the latter half of the 1960s, Labour had lost a series of by-elections, as might be expected in mid-administration. However, the situation became so serious that we were in danger of losing overall control of the council in the foreseeable future. We had to stop the rot and show that we could win, give people confidence in us again, as the success of our policies just was not being translated into votes.

A by-election came up in the very marginal ward of Pitsea; we just could not afford to lose it. An elderly chap called George Hurd considered standing as an Independent Labour candidate. He was well known locally as the chairman of the old people's community at Vange and Pitsea. Pitsea had a predominantly elderly population.

Along with another party member, Ken Stone, I approached George and asked if he would stand as the Labour candidate instead. He said that he would on condition that he was made chairman of the welfare committee. There was no way that I could agree to this, but I was prepared to give him a seat on the committee. He settled for that, but was not prepared to join the Labour Party, as he had been a lifetime member of the Independent Labour Party, and found it hard to resign. Ken was very persuasive, however, and managed to get a year's subscription out of George, though to the best of my knowledge he never paid again.

George won the seat, and the future of the Labour group looked more secure for the immediate future. I made no apologies about this, it was necessary for us to keep control, because we were the only party with the sufficient will to fight central government and the BDC in order to push through the policies that were giving the people of Basildon a decent place to live and work in. Basildon enjoyed the fruits of George Hurd's conversion.

The new senior citizen's centre, the brainchild of Cyril Thirkettle, was named after George Hurd when he died. This was partly in recognition of his work on behalf of the elderly, but mainly to serve the dual purpose of recognising how he got the Labour Group out of a hole and to strengthen the association between the elderly voters and the Labour Pary; showing the benefits like the centre that voting correctly accrued.

139

But it was Cyril Thirkettle who spent months and months researching and preparing reports for the Labour Group on the centre. I apologise to him, in justice it should have been the Cyril Thirkettle Centre. But the building itself and the idea behind it are perhaps a tribute to Cyril's hard work in themselves. I was able to redress this lack of recognition by a letter to the local press many years ago, but it is nice to be able to salute his efforts in print again.

All in all though, my reputation for being incorruptible remained intact, which prevented most of the big boys from going too far in trying to entice me to give them contracts. Nevertheless, I was approached a number of times by the large building companies with substantial bribes. They were sensible enough not to push the point any further when I refused a share in their ill-gotten gains. They knew I could not be bought.

When I have wondered about the phrase 'every man has his price', I have normally brought to mind the rumours that have circulated about the sort of sums taken by some Labour councillors in the 1980s. I then wonder if these exorbitant figures would have tempted me — I am glad to say I never had the chance to find out.

Yet Labour was not alone in enjoying the benefits of palm greasing: one of the few Tories that I liked was Terry Chapman, who became leader of the council after the 1968 election. We got on well together, in spite of the fact that I was certain that he was constantly up to all sorts of shady deals. He was abusing his position as a councillor for sure. He was also involved in some deals of a very dubious nature with David Taylor and some market traders, but nothing illegal was ever proved there. In the end his downfall was the traditional Tory temptation — sex, or rather, abusing his council perks to obtain sex.

Terry took two of the female council staff with him on a conference, with the intention of having a sex orgy. The two girls concerned booked their time at the conference in with the council. I got wind of what had taken place. I reported the girls and then spoke to Terry. 'You either resign or we'll make an issue of this in the council chamber. My boys are not prepared to keep quiet about it.'

Terry resigned. I got on well with him, but I would not tolerate such flagrant misuse of the public's money, besides which, I figured it was a case of guilty with about a good two dozen other offences to be taken into consideration. A few months afterwards he was killed in a car accident in Prague, and I was very sorry, Tory villain or no Tory villain.

How strange it is that so many of the council from that time passed away within a short space of time of each other. Some had done financially well out of their membership, while others, Labour and Tory, had struggled along, well-meaning people doing their best for the community, and with not a penny to show for it. It would not have crossed their minds to take a bribe, yet it would have been easy for them to do so and end up like the other fat cats.

One of the first greed motivated men I came up against was Bill Davis, a builder's merchant. Before I became leader of Basildon all building workers used by the council had to go to Davis's shop to buy all their materials for a job, and I mean all, right down to the screws and nails. Bill Davis was chairman of works for the council.

Charlie Weston, on the other hand, was chairman of establishment, which maintained official council buildings and offices. Council, clerical and white-collar workers were so pleased when Charlie agreed to refurbish their offices every six months. This was costing the rent payers a bomb. It was only after the 1963 election that I realised that he owned one of the biggest furniture shops in Wickford. I will leave you to work out where all the council furniture was supplied from. I quickly put an end to that over-expenditure and waste of public funds.

Sometimes the abuse of position was a little more subtle, but I was still able to ferret it out, because once you gain a reputation for rooting out cheats, people know they can come to you in the knowledge that you will root out the problem.

Such a case concerned one of the motor dealers in town. Every year they held a barbecue, at which there was a raffle with fabulous prizes on offer, such as trips to Majorca. Every year the Town Manager and the Transport Manager either ended up improving their tans or taking away some highly desirable prize. Once again, I will leave it to your deductive powers to work out why the executive official of the town and the official responsible for buying cars continually won superb prizes in a game of chance at a large motor dealers.

I was told of this annual raffle, and did some putting of two and two together. When it made four I bided my time. Then one year I was invited to the barbecue.

I was standing with the owner of the dealership when David Taylor came up to me and said 'Oh, how glad I am to see you here'.

'Glad to be here. There's just one thing, if either you or the manager win the raffle tonight, you can both look for a job on Monday morning.'

There was a look of consternation on everyone's faces, accompanied by hurried whispered conversations. Lo and behold, the raffle was delayed for some unknown reason. When it was finally picked, there were a couple of genuinely delighted people who had never expected to win, to say nothing of a few red faces for those who shortly before were sure they would win.

141

I was shrewd enough and powerful enough to take on the spivs and con merchants of Basildon, but I think I bit off more than I could chew when I took on Prince Philip over his Duke of Edinburgh Award Scheme: at least I think I did, because there was a strange and sinister incident that happened not long after my objection to the way the scheme was being run, and although I believe in coincidences, I still think that 'someone' high up decided to shake me up a little.

It started in 1963 when I first noticed how poorly funded the scheme seemed to be at local level, which was reducing the effectiveness of what I considered to be an important programme for the young people of Basildon. The more I investigated the funding of the scheme, the more suspicious I was of where some of the money was going.

That December I wrote to Prince Philip direct, and received a typically snooty reply from his secretary, one Rear-Admiral Christopher Bonham-Carter, C.B., C.V.O., which informed me that my letter had been passed on to the awards office. It also assured me that central finances were 'a constant source of concern'. Then came the sting, which said that it was quite easy for me to write that something should be done to see that funds were raised, but more difficult to do; was it not up to those who thought the scheme worthwhile to see that something was done to stop the awards from failing?

In other words, I and others like me should have been doing their job for them. I did not need somebody with more letters in their name than a Scrabble set to tell me to get off my backside when those who were paid to do the job were failing to pull their weight.

I was contacted by Sir John Hunt, who was running the awards on the Duke's behalf. Eventually I got to meet him at his offices in London.

As I was complaining to him about what I saw as the waste of money on central administration, I noticed that he had a large typing pool, staffed entirely by a type of girl once known as Sloane Rangers; none of them seemed to be very taxed by their work.

'Why have you got all these tarts here pretending to work for you?' I delicately enquired.

'What did you call them?'

'You heard me.'

And everyone else in the building I suspect, the volume control on my vocal chords has been stuck on 'loud' since those days of having to shout above all those other little Morgan mouths in the kitchen at Canning Town. Sir John and I parted on less than friendly terms, with nothing resolved. I had hinted at 'jobs for the girls', and I think that touched a nerve, not out of indignation, but fear of being exposed.

The sinister part occurred as I was at home, preparing to go out to a council meeting. There was a knock at the door, and I answered, finding two plainly dressed men on my step.

'We want to come in and search your house. You can't deny us entry; we are Customs and Excise — we don't need a warrant.'

I was flabbergasted, but quickly recovered my senses.

'You hang on here a minute, you're not coming in.'

'You can't stop us.'

They barged past me. I went straight to the telephone and called the police. I explained the situation, and they amazed me by confirming that these two men did not require a warrant to enter my home.

However, a squad car was duly sent round, and the police had a word outside with the two 'customs men'. Then the officers came over to me and again confirmed that my uninvited guests had every right to do what they were doing.

The two men then proceeded to methodically turn my place upside down. Chris collapsed in tears. I tried to ask them what it was all about, but they would not reply. I gave them an ultimatum.

'If you don't tell me, then I'm telling you now I'm going to use physical force — and I can do it. I don't give a damn — I'll use physical force on you now.'

'We have reason to believe that you've been involved in arson in the East End of London — burning down three factories.'

I could not credit it. I felt funny inside. Then they found a piece of paper that Chris had written on. It read 'half a dozen slips, half a dozen jumpers.' One of them turned to me: 'This connects you with one of the clothing warehouses that has been burnt down. It's been burnt down by the owners, and you're involved with it.'

'How can I be involved with it?'

'Well we believe you are.'

'I'm going to get a solicitor. Now out you go, you haven't found what you're looking for — I don't know what you're looking for.'

After about two hours they did eventually leave. When I told them to put all of our stuff back and clear up the hell of a mess they had left, they just told me that I watched too many television programmes. I asked the police to come back and take a look at the state of the place.

'We don't want to know; we don't get involved with those people.'

I went to see a solicitor the following day. He spent a total of three months trying to find out what the intrusion was all about, but to no avail. It turned out that some factories had burnt down in the East End. I found their details out, and they were all owned by some Greeks I had never even heard of.

Nobody in authority has contacted me about that case ever since, neither Customs and Excise or the police, Whoever the two men were, they certainly were not from customs. I was shaken at the time, but on reflection I realised that if they were warning me off then surely they should have followed it up, but they never did. If it was someone in a government department giving orders then I am not surprised that I was not contacted again, it would be a typical cock-up of Whitehall's not to follow through on something they had started. I still cannot be one hundred percent sure that was the intention of the visit, but it certainly boded ill for the liberty of the public, as other cases since have shown; although I am sure that no-one at the helm of the Duke of Edinburgh scheme in any way was involved.

Another case that stank the moment I heard about it was a little scandal involving an ex-England cricketer. He had been given a warehouse at Pitsea Marshes, at the discretion of the Basildon council estates officer. Nothing wrong in that by itself.

What put me on to the case was a telephone call I received from an Asian businessman. He claimed that he had applied for the unit first, and had paid the rent. This was duly returned when the cricketer was given the warehouse. I smelt a rat. I guessed that the estates officer had taken a bribe. The reason I was so quick to jump to this conclusion was primarily that I had always had serious doubts about the estates officer's honesty, but nothing discriminating had ever come to light.

When I questioned him about the whole affair he gave me a cock and bull story about the businessman having not paid his rent on time, which meant he had to let the warehouse go to the cricketer, who was second in the queue. I interviewed everyone involved, but none of the explanations I received were satisfactory, so I suspended the estates officer pending an enquiry.

At the enquiry it became painfully obvious that the businessman had been entitled to the warehouse, but for reasons never fully substantiated, the cricketer was given the tenancy instead.

Accordingly I overruled the allocation, and took the tenancy away and restored it to the original tenant. I then had a call from a solicitor threatening to take action against the council.

'Go ahead, it'll be interesting to see what comes out in court.'

No action was taken against the council, and I have heard nothing else from the solicitor to date.

The estates officer was sacked, but appealed against the dismissal. NALGO, his union, withdrew the appeal after they studied the facts of the case, and ended up accepting that his dismissal was entirely fair.

Entirely fair is hardly a phrase one could associate with Batchelor when it came to ballots. I caught him out when he tried to use his switching tactics on me, but I let him off the hook because I allowed my judgement to be swayed by personal consideration. He probably would not even had dared tried it if I had not decided to make Bill Archibald my successor as party leader.

My year as leader had come to an end. I discussed with Alf Dove who would be the best successor for the party. We decided to pick on someone weak, in order that I could become Town Chairman and control them. I could return to being party leader at the end of my year as Chairman. It seemed the best way to deflect Potter and Tinworth's attacks on me, and I would return with more support than ever.

'We don't want anyone strong because he would make his mark on the group, and you want to get the job back as leader,' Alf pointed out.

So we decided on Bill Archibald. He was the sort of chap we could control. We spoke to him about the post, and he was chosen. If only I could have foreseen at the time that if I could control Bill, there was every reason to suspect that Potter and Tinworth might try to do the same; they were certainly strong enough in Basildon by now.

And control him they did, and he allowed them and Batchelor to bend and break every rule in the book. I was more or less power- less to stop them, because I did not even get to be made leader again.

I then went around group members, canvassing votes. My returns showed that I had a clear majority, and would be elected leader. I lost to, guess who? Bill Archibald, by four votes, and was shocked, to say the least. Who had betrayed me or lied? My canvassing showed that I should have won by four votes. That figure should have told me all I needed to know.

Immediately afterwards I went against the decision of Archibald to ban me from chairing any of the council committees. Because I opposed the decision, it had to go to a vote. I won by a majority of four, which confirmed exactly the support I knew I had from the outset. Now I was suspicious.

I went to Batchelor and asked if I could see the ballot papers for the leadership. He refused.

I called a meeting of my people, and they all came round to my house, the only place I now felt was safe from Potter's influence. We resolved to re-canvass all the members who said they had voted for me. When we did, all of them swore blind that they had put their cross beside the name Morgan. George Elder had been my ally at Barstable ward for a long time, he suggested that we went up to Transport House and asked for an enquiry.

He and I accordingly went up to London and had an interview with Reg Underhill, the party's local government officer. Not only did I tell him about the leadership vote, but I decided that I had to explain the Bob Chaplin incident as well, whatever the consequences might be.

Reg telephone Batchelor, and fortunately he got through to him while George and I were still in the room. Reg told Batchelor to present the ballot papers in order to clear the matter up. When mention was made of the Chaplin affair, Batchelor merely denied all knowledge. He went on to say that he had destroyed the ballot papers, to which Reg responded by telling him that he would report the matter to the executive council, who in turn would invalidate the election.

He added that he would contact Batchelor again to discuss the matter, but did not want to talk any further in front of George and myself.

'What do I do now?' I asked.

'I think you could well ask for another meeting of the group and a new vote. If this is refused then I believe that I, as party local government officer would have to take it up, and have an enquiry or force a new vote.'

'What do you think would happen then?'

'Well, they'll vote.'

'No, I don't mean that. But party members would be upset by my forcing another vote, and it's possible that I would lose in any case. I could take the risk, but I don't know. I don't know what to do yet, I'll let you know.'

But Reg was obviously concerned about the Chaplin vote rigging, and said that I would have to put the allegation in writing for there to be an enquiry into Batchelor's tenure of secretary agent.

'I don't know, I've never trusted paid officers of the party, no disrespect to you Reg, but when it comes to it, they all stick together.'

'No they won't. Not if we find that there has been a misuse of secretary agent's powers.'

'But how do I prove it? The other councillors won't back me, or get involved in it. As for Archibald and Alf Dove, they certainly wouldn't support me on this. They would deny it and put it down to sour grapes on my part. No, leave it. Sod 'em!'

I did not budge from that decision, I remained obstinate and wrong on the issue. I should have asked for a full enquiry, but I suppose my wish always to be liked coupled with not wanting more dissention in the party had the final say. But I vowed I would get my own back, somehow.

Even then I did not fully realise the strength of Potter and Tinworth, now that Batchelor was fixing things for them. They would hold private meetings in Potter's and Batchelor's houses, plotting and planning my downfall. It was not enough that I was not leader, they wanted me and my supporters out of the picture completely. My councillors were going to be replaced by those who thought only right-wing policies would win elections, and who considered it their right to grow rich at the expense of the rent and rate payers, claiming inflated expenses and earning from Quango appointments.

Getting proof in this climate was the most difficult thing, strange meetings and friendships were there for all to see, but evidence that would stand up in a court of law was an elusive goal in my campaign against those who had hi-jacked the Party.

Some who had been caught with their palms still sticky tried to bluff it out, and if they were lucky they sometimes got away with it. Not so Johnny Blake. Again, it had come to my attention that someone was on the take. A builder accused Johnny, a councillor, of taking bent money.

'Johnny, either prosecute the builder who's made these accusations against you, or resign.'

'Oh, I'm going to prosecute.'

The following morning, slipped underneath my door was a letter from Johnny, saying that he had decided to retire because of ill health. I liked Johnny, and might have been tempted to do a 'Costello' and cover up for him, but like many others, some of whom, like Johnny, were good and able councillors, he fell into temptation. His trouble was that he had been caught, others were normally more clever.

Johnny was a great character and I was shocked when his wife telephoned me to tell me of his death by heart attack. He was so full of life and ideas most of them so over the top, others were brilliant but always seemed to end in failure for Johnny, but others took them over and made a mint. One such scheme was for a Greyhound Racing Track in Basildon's Gloucester Park. It entailed dog track and totaliser, sports, athletics and restaurant.

Johnny came to me with the idea and I suggested he raised it at a planning meeting. He was then given the go ahead to look into the project much to the annoyance of the Treasurer and the Chief Engineer who felt it should be their remit.

Johnny came to me a few weeks later to say he had made contact with two brothers from the East End of London named

Lupas. They had the controlling interest in Clapton Dog Track (now closed down). I suggested Johnny continued negotiations without any commitments.

It was a few weeks later that Tom Driberg telephoned me at the council offices, Roy Homewood later to become Assistant Town Manager was present. (Roy was my No. 1 adviser behind the scenes.) Tom had heard through 'channels' that we (the council) were contemplating building a Greyhound Track and he suggested that he knew a couple of financiers who would be interested in the project. I told him my Chairman of planning was discussing this with two brothers, namely Lupas of Clapton Stadium. Tom suggested that a meet could be advantageous and suggested a venue of White City Dog Track. I made some excuse and suggested he rang me back in a couple of days. This he never did.

A few days later Johnny came to a meeting and put forward a scheme where finances would be made available to build a stadium at NO cost to the council.

The backers would bear all costs and would have full control of (A) the totaliser for 25 years and (B) the restaurant for 25 years. They would then give control to the Council.

Members of the Labour Group supported this on the whole. Some had misgivings but agreed to a meeting by Johnny, myself, the Treasurer and the Chief Engineer. The meeting to be held at, surprise, surprise, White City Dog Track. Immediately the Labour members departed the meeting, I collared Johnny and asked him if Tom Driberg had been in contact with him. Johnny was genuinely surprised and stated that he did not know or have any contacts with Driberg. He ended up by saying 'Why should someone so high up as Driberg contact me?' I enquired who had suggested White City Dog Track and Johnny replied 'The Clapton Stadium crowd'.

A few days before the White City meeting, urgent Council business came up and I could not attend. I forget who stood in for me. But on the Monday morning the Council Treasurer asked to see me. He was very agitated and claimed that he was shocked at being sent to a meeting where underworld figures were present discussing financial propositions with Basildon.

I placated him and assured him I would get a full explanation from Johnny Blake.

I telephone Johnny and told him to report to my office. Johnny wore his usual feigned look of hurt at suggestions that the people who he had met up with were well known villains. He said he only knew the two Lupas brothers and they had two friends, also brothers who Johnny was sure were never introduced. They were, said

Johnny, 'two gentlemen' who were also interested in investing money into Basildon's Greyhound Stadium.

I told Johnny in his and everyone's interest the project should be dropped. I then suggested to the Treasurer that he produce a report that it was not a financially viable project. He was not happy about this but I was able to persuade him that it was in his own interest to do it that way.

To this day I can only speculate about Driberg's influence and who were the financiers. It is now a well known fact that Driberg, through his homosexual contacts, was well in with villains in London's East and South East End and they probably wanted the stadium as a front or for laundering money.

This then was Johnny Blake, a colourful character who after leaving the council went on to open one of Basildon's first Pub and Night Clubs 'The Van Gogh'.

Johnny was a creator with the brains and imagination that should have been used and utilised, but again he was an East End kid and the so-called middle class intellectuals sneered at him and often took him for a ride after hijacking his ideas.

Clever enough to cover their tracks, for sure. I was once sent a dossier on a Labour councillor which alleged various things, such as meetings at the home of a Tory ex-councillor, where he had met up with David Taylor and a certain builder. The builder had been linked with Taylor after the Municipal Journal had accused Taylor of corruption. The dossier went on to make several accusations about the intent of these meetings and the motives of those involved, but nothing it contained could be substantiated.

When it came to some other councillors, again it was patently obvious something was amiss, but documentation was hard to come by. The most obvious example being the relationship between the council and a certain building company.

The company had a terrible name around town because some of the houses they had built that later fell down. I was amazed when after all that they were given another contract, and a very unusual one at that.

Basildon Council had drawn up a continuous contract, that would carry on even if their original contract houses started to deteriorate badly. The council had in fact accepted a compensation deal from them over the question of defective buildings, conditional on the company's name and the site of any sub-standard houses never being published.

Now why on earth would a council like Basildon agree to protect a builder in such a manner as would raise public concern were it generally known? Of course, there is nothing that directly links this deal to anything underhand. But no-one can deny this is a very strange deal indeed.

John Costello was a different kettle of fish altogether. He was a character, liked and idolised by many. A huge, fat man with a presence to match. He still cared about the people, got out on the streets and sorted their problems for them. He did not look down on them as a bunch of cattle who should be grateful for his existence in their proximity. Unfortunately, he thought this entitled him to more than his fair share of life's riches and pleasures. He held high office, including that of Town Chairman.

When he died I was asked to say a few words at his funeral. John was a Catholic, but that was as far as it went, so despite his popularity, I and some others were surprised to see the church host to a packed congregation. It seemed like some sort of comfort for the grieving widow, Rene Costello.

I had hardly finished saying my piece when two police officers arrived with a warrant to stop the funeral. Confusion reigned before it was announced that the corpse was to be confiscated by the police. We started to file out, and what happened next can only be explained by what I found out afterwards regarding the stopping of the funeral.

It transpired that John had another wife hidden away somewhere, and she had now turned up to claim her husband's body and estate. Rene Costello had been masquerading as his wife for years, but they had never been married because John had not divorced his first wife. Rene herself was a respected county councillor, and had served on Basildon council as well. Would she now be left virtually penniless?

Not as long as John's friends were around. John had large sums of money hidden in his house, and it was alleged that a certain man, who went on to become a councillor made sure he got to it before the authorities did. Those involved must have wondered why such large sums were not in the bank, but I think that it was no more than malicious gossip.

I was a social worker by this time, having left the council behind me to serve the community in a different way. And it was as a social worker some time before that I came across a case involving a certain councillor.

I had to visit a woman who had been neglecting her child. As soon as I arrived she made accusations against the councillor, saying he had visited her house and had sex with her. She further claimed that the wife had come round and caught them together, which ended with the councillor being hit all the way home with an umbrella. The picture that conjured up still makes me laugh now.

I once attended a conference in the Isle of Man with John in our council capacity. On the flight over, a certain Tory knight and M.P., who was also attending (though in his case his capacity was more concerned with alcohol) sat next to me. This was unpleasant enough, but as the quite short flight proceeded he proceeded as well — to get drunk. Then he started to fondle one of the hostesses as she walked past. I told him to stop it, and that I thought he was a dirty old b...., but he did not seem to take much notice of a man who was merely a clothcap socialist. If only his constituents could have seen how he was behaving.

We arrived on Man and checked into our hotel, where John picked up with a woman from Blackpool. He promised to marry her and goodness knows what else. I told him not to be a fool, that he ought to guard his position as a councillor, but he paid as much attention as the Tory knight. Whether John was aware of it or not, this woman kept hold of his pyjamas after we left.

Bob Hurley, a reporter on the Basildon Standard, called me up to ask if I knew which councillor the pyjamas, a woman had sent the paper, belonged to.

'Well just look at the size of them and guess.'

He did, and everyone in the newsroom roared out 'John Costello'. This was a source of great mirth in the local press circles for a long time after the scandal.

On a more worrying note, there was another sex scandal which John got involved in, though he was not the one caught with his trousers around his ankles.

A young girl claimed that a leading figure in the local party had under-age sex with her. She named the individual concerned, who later went on to be a top civic members, as he still is at the time of writing (1992). John Costello asked the girl to put her accusation in writing. Whether he ever used this piece of poison for blackmail, I do not know; but it is difficult to believe that having gone to the trouble of obtaining a written incrimination of someone, he left it lying at the bottom of a desk drawer.

One thing is for sure, John Costello was a one off, some would say amen to that, but he certainly was a character and a half, and I thought the world of him, villain or not.

I had to smile to myself again when I realised what a shock a certain councillor must have had when he realised Joe Morgan was the case social worker for the woman he had sex with. There was another twist to that story, for the woman actually came from Majorca, and ended up demanding a house in Basildon or her air fair back home. I had to categorically tell her that she could not expect to get her air fare paid. Eventually I had to take her child into care.

151

The county council felt in rather an awkward position, and were not quite sure how to react. Firstly, they tried to pressure me to leave the councillor's name out of my case file, but I pointed out that it was too late, his name had been mentioned, it definitely was him, and his name would be going on file. At this point high powered officials got involved, and to avoid further disconcert they arranged for the woman to be paid by the DHSS to fly back to Majorca.

So here we have a case of a government department paying tax-payers' money for a private foreign individual to fly back to Majorca, where she had a flat, purely because a councillor let his groin rule his brain. The child was bundled from reception to care, then back to her mother, who could then quite happily carry on disregarding her responsibilities to her own flesh and blood.

One person who as far as I know never accepted money, and certainly never behaved in the fashion John did, was Alf Dove. We had more or less started off together in local politics, so I grew to know him pretty well. He was a nice chap to know, but as a politician he did not command anybody's respect, because Alf was only interested in backing the winners of any power struggle. That was why he was solidly behind me when I was in power, but swearing allegiance to the new order the second I had left. Apart from briefly sitting as an independent during the left-wing right-wing rows before Labour gained power in Basildon, he never stuck his neck out. He was always right behind you, but he was never first out of the trenches.

Alf was a survivor, and I knew this. So it was perhaps with this at the back of my mind that I entered a room in the council offices that Alf, Eric Batchelor and Bill Archibald had asked me along to. This was during a Labour group meeting, so everyone who was anyone was next door.

Batchelor spoke first.

'We need to get Chaplin off the council.'

'Why's that?'

'Because he's becoming more and more of an embarrassment with his court cases. He's coming up again very soon.'

'Who says so?'

Batchelor produced an official looking paper.

'Look,' I started, 'I'm not taking any part in your tricks again.'

'Well this court case that's coming up could help to destroy the group.'

They then all pleaded with me to help them get Bob Chaplin expelled from the party. When I asked on what grounds they were going to kick him out, Batchelor replied, 'that's easy'.

It was then that I realised that the three of them had already discussed this in some detail previously, because their plan was already complete. They figured they would tell me at the last moment.

The plan was childishly simple and sure to work. All we had to do was find an item that Bob would definitely speak on, and then ban him from doing so. The group whip would be put on him, but Bob was sure to insist on speaking anyway, that was the sort of chap he was. When he spoke he would be breaking the party whip, which was sufficient grounds to have him expelled from the group, if not the party. I refused to take any part in it. This was when Batchelor wheeled out his master stroke.

'Remember Joe, although you didn't take part, you kept quiet when we rigged the vote at the constituency meeting.'

(Dove and Archibald were not to my knowledge involved in the original vote rigging.)

I looked at the three of them in disgust. They knew I was in a corner. I asked for a few minutes to think it over. There was no way out: either I would have to expose the lot of them, and the fact that I had tacitly supported the vote rigging by keeping quiet, something the Labour Party would not forgive easily, or I could go along with them.

So an item was found, something on the rents in Bob's ward. He was duly told that he was not to speak on the subject, and as expected he ignored the whip, because that was the sort of fellow he was. A special meeting was called which expelled him from the group, after which he resigned from the party. After that I barely ever spoke to Batchelor.

David Taylor as Town Manager was the idol of the business groups in Basildon. Yet in my opinion he betrayed everything he claimed to be: socialist, man of the workers and an anti-Tory. He believed that no-one could tell him what to do or how to do it in Basildon; he had all the answers. His style of self-publicity and brash, rash pronouncements would have been acceptable if he had produced results to match, but in my opinion he failed to fulfil the expectations I had of his role, and fell even shorter of his own grandiose claims; what a tragedy for Basildon that Alma Hatt did not live a few years longer, and set a precedent for what a town manager could do. All David was really interested in was playing golf, being a Rotarian and going out to dinner.

David and myself were the main speakers at an annual dinner of the Basildon Golf Society. Why they invited me, their biggest enemy, I'm not sure. Perhaps they thought I would be shown up.

David spoke first, going on and on about his favourite subject — David Taylor:

'Some people believe that I can walk on water, but I am just like you, my friends out there.'

He sat down to warm applause, having massaged their egos and his own. I rose to speak, deliberately looking round for 20 or 30 seconds before announcing 'I will be brief'. Cries of 'good', and 'hear hear' greeted me. I thanked them for inviting Chris and me to the dinner. Then I turned my attention to David.

'David has given you a glowing report on Basildon; he also said people believe that he can walk on water. Well, he can — because I give him permission to do so.'

I then sat down, there was initially a silence for some seconds, followed by roars of laughter and long, loud clapping. The rest of the evening was a resounding success, with people coming up and saying well done.

From then on I had regular invites to the Golf Society's dinner, though I doubt they ever completely forgave me for making the new golf course a municipal one.

David Taylor took early retirement at 50, and he went on to become a county councillor. When he left the post of town manager there were mumbles of a planning application fiddle involving a grocery chain but again, if anything had happened at all, then the tracks had been covered, so this was just so much rumour. All I know is that when he died a few years later, he left a large estate, a very large estate. So large that no-one could ever tie up where he had earned it all from. Those who have succeeded him as town manager have merely gone about building a little empire, a sinecure that harks back to the old style town clerk, which was precisely what I was trying to get away from.

Meanwhile, in 1973 I gave Potter his chance on a plate when the national issue of housing Ugandan Asians came to Basildon New Town. Even now I wonder how I could have fallen into Potter's trap.

Central government had asked local councils to house a number of Ugandan Asians who had been expelled from Idi Amin's dictatorship. Basildon was to house some of these families. This was a straightforward request which had no need to appear on any agenda; but Potter decided otherwise. Word had got back to him that a couple of my stalwarts were bitterly opposed to the idea of letting immigrants have priority over local people. I had no such misgivings myself, but Potter saw his chance and set off to tackle Bill Archibald, our amiable but naïve council leader.

Potter successfully argued that the Asian Ugandan matter be put on the agenda of the next meeting for debate. He knew this would cause at least one of the dissenters — Mick Crew — to rebel if the issue went public. I would be tarred with the same brush and forced into a corner. Bill Archibald was too ingenuous and straightforward, and under Potter's sway, to see any motive in this move, even though he should have dismissed the idea in view of the fact that it could only lead to dissention, and further, the chairman of housing, Ron Austin, was quite prepared to sympathetically handle the matter and house the Asians with a minimum of fuss and publicity.

Bear in mind that we were talking about just a few houses in national terms which were to be given to people thrown out of their own country on the whim of a madman; we were not talking about turning over a whole estate at a moment's notice on the say so of some hare-brained government scheme. Mick Crew failed to recognise this, but Potter did not. But he also realised that he could make a huge issue out of what was essentially a not terribly important matter. I knew that only five at most of the Labour group were against the scheme, so this was not some great rebellion. If there had been no debate there would have only been mild rumblings of discontent, but nothing more.

In any case, I tried to avert a split by offering a compromise to Mick and the others: the idea being to house the Asian families, but to make their priority on the list one, three, five, seven, nine and eleven, thus allowing local people already on the list to be placed two, four and so forth on the list. This seemed a fair way to go about things, with neither side being discriminated against, Basildon residents would not be kept waiting for ages on the list, and the Asian families would not come into an atmosphere of resentment. Certainly Mick and the others thought so. Ron Austin agreed to the proposal being put forth at the meeting.

This did not make much difference, because Potter immediately launched into every predictable cliché about the idea smacking of racism. He made his accusations acute enough to annoy Mick and the others as a prelude to the vote. Tempers flared. Of course, the vote had little to do with the Asian issue, it was really Morgan against Potter.

When the proposal was defeated by two votes, it was no surprise that Mick Crew resigned from the party and the council. Unfortunately he then chose to stand as an anti-Asian candidate in the ensuing by-election, even after members of the Barstable ward who were loyal to me begged him not to. This particularly disgusted me: Mick playing straight into Potter's hands. I could see what Potter's intent was, but Mick managed to do all his dirty work for him by being pig-headed.

Then Batchelor called a completely illegal ward meeting to pick an official Labour candidate to stand for the by-election. He did not invite the stalwarts of the ward or the executive, instead he filled the meeting with people who were stooges, some of them not even in the Labour Party. Such a person was Mary Smith, who had not paid subscriptions to the ward party for the past three years. This was not because she had left of her own accord, rather that the ward would not collect her money after it was alleged that she was somehow involved with the loss of funds collected for a children's Christmas party which had to be cancelled. In mitigation of Mary, I would mention that I found out later that she had paid her dues direct to party headquarters. I squashed those allegations at my earliest convenience. Yet she and others of a similarly high standing were turning out to a place they had no right to be in to vote for who should represent a political party they did not belong to.

I complained most bitterly about this flagrant coup to Batchelor. He could only say that it was a properly constituted meeting and that was all there was to it. This was a straightforward lie, and I pointed out that people who had attended the meeting were not even party members. He ignored this, and Bill Archibald and the others let him get away with it.

I should not have been surprised at these tactics. Batchelor and Potter used the idea of ringers who would bleat in their support before. They had decided from the start that the only way to defeat the 'cloth cap' element was to get rid of it. But they knew they did not have the numbers inside the party willing to support them, so they began dragging in anyone who would do their bidding. It sounds incredible, but it is true.

Only the month before Mick resigned, Batchelor had allowed two people to go onto the council, neither of whom was in the Labour Party. He only enrolled them the night they took their seats. In fact one of them never even paid his subscription.

If you think that is just ridiculous, you should have been with me when I went canvassing a couple of years afterwards. One of the men concerned was a worker at the Ford tractor factory, and he lived in the Kingswood area. I knocked at his door and asked if we could count on his vote.

'No, I don't vote Labour.'

'But you were a Labour councillor,' I protested.

'I was asked to consider becoming a councillor. When I told him I wasn't a member of the party he said it didn't matter, he said he'd get me a ticket and then I could become a councillor.'

This is exactly how Potter was managing to orchestrate trouble for me, he had his sheep behind him ready to bleat and support anything he said, after all, they were getting paid.

All the wrangling and lying over selection for the official candidate did not militate well, and Mick Crew duly won the election. Whether this was Batchelor's intention or not, Potter and he had succeeded in splitting their own party and council group.

156

Potter had accomplished step one of his scheme to get rid of me and Bill Archibald.

Then the original issue came before the council — whether to house the Asians or not. The Tories, and four Labour councillors voted against the scheme. I though my best plan was to abstain, because I had no intention of backing Potter, so I did not vote.

Of course, Potter immediately demanded for action to be taken against those who had broken the party whip. The four who voted with the opposition were given six weeks suspension. I had only abstained, but was handed down an indefinite suspension. I was amazed, to say the least. I immediately appealed to Transport House, who decided to hold their own enquiry. But far from getting to the truth of the matter, their methods of questioning and withholding information merely turned the whole thing into a farce.

At once stage Potter and Batchelor handed the enquiry team a lengthy report of their own, saying 'we do not wish Morgan to know what is in the report'. The enquiry team, three elderly dodderers, as judge and jury, read the report before telling Batchelor that they could not accept the contents unless they could be shown to me. Batchelor refused to concede, and amazingly, the team gave in, and just said it would disregard the report. Yet they had now read the contents of the report, so even the most objective of them could not entirely disregard what it said when they came to make their final decision. Common justice dictates that they should never have read the report in the first place, at least until they had assurances that I could see what it contained.

The judgement from Transport House was that my suspension be altered from indefinite to six months. I really lost my temper and resigned straightaway. Potter had achieved step two: the council and Joe Morgan were now strangers.

Two aspects of differing but equally interesting matters came to light some time afterwards: the first, a year later, was of some comfort to me on a personal note. I was talking to someone who had made a study of racial prejudice about the Asian Ugandan housing issue. After carefully taking in the facts of the case, he told me that certain individuals, who had pushed the issue under the noses of the public, were using the refugees for their own ends, and therefore had little genuine interest in the welfare of those they were pretending to champion. In his opinion, they were even more racist than the likes of Mick Crew who had made a racially controversial speech at that time. It might only be an academic opinion, but it made me feel a lot better, especially when you consider that the 'councillor' from Kingswood was an Asian chap; Potter, in my opinion, had picked the man's colour to build his own image up and further his own ambitions. If that is not racism then I do not know what is.

The second, and on a wider scale, more important matter was the Transport House enquiry report which Eric Moonman managed to obtain just before he was ditched as M.P., when he failed to measure up to Potter's expectations. It made interesting reading — the whole enquiry was a complete travesty, a farrago of downright lies and individual opinions that bore hardly any semblance of the true events. Quotes from newspaper articles on the matter were attributed to me, when I had copies of the actual articles that proved the words were mouthed by another Labour councillor, Ken Tyson. Potter and Batchelor had somehow managed to wind the enquiry team, who could not even get their facts right, around their grubby little fingers.

Eric felt we had an ideal opportunity to appeal, but I queried whether it was all worth it. What Eric and I did not know at the time was that the plan to dump him was already under way. He made the same mistake as me, in that he thought he could take Potter and the rest of them on, and he trusted the wrong people, that is, those who went on to betray him. But like me, Eric was a volatile character, and he resigned from the party rather than fight his corner.

I was feeling low and very sorry for myself when I arrived home after resigning, and I tried to cheer myself up with the prospect of the three week holiday I was taking the family on the next day. I told myself that I had worked hard and saved what I could from my work as an insurance agent to earn this holiday and I should make the most of the Yugoslavian sunshine on offer. In any case, I was just developing angina in 1973, and I had seen a few councillors collapse in the chamber and later die of a heart attack. I did not want to be just another political stress statistic. Perhaps I was better off out of it altogether, I reasoned as I boarded the airliner.

When I arrived back, I decided to apply to the county council for a job as a social worker. Here was an opportunity to divert my energies into somewhere removed from the stupidity and skulduggery of politics, or so I thought. I was successful, even though the Tory-controlled council knew exactly who I was and what I stood for.

What I did not know was that they appointed me in the face of a 50-strong petition from the social services section which objected to my coming to work with them. I only found out ten years later, when it came to light that the person who had initiated the petition was now a big friend of mine! If I had known at the time how the lie of the land was, I do not think I would have stayed, so low had my confidence been since being suspended by Transport House.

I steered clear of the Basildon Labour Party for some time, but when I realised that there were still enough people in it who were honest enough to make the organisation worthwhile. I remembered something a very old socialist told me, 'there's nothing wrong with the Labour Party, it's just some of the people in it that are no good'. And that just about sums it up. Besides, there was no other party who would fight for the people's rights and needs properly. And I still wanted to fight on and try and achieve at least some fraction of the dream for the town I had started out with. I had taken my turn in the front line, but I was prepared to back others who would carry on the attack against bureaucracy an injustice.

So I went back to the party and the people, and started to earn their respect a gain, but from now on, social work took precedence over politics.

Chapter Eleven
'FATHER JOE'

And so I went back to the party and earned the respect of the people, enabling me to look at others with contempt, and they knew it. One day, I was sure, they would be found out.

But still Potter and Tinworth tried to dog me: when I needed to sell my house the solicitor made a mistake which meant that at the last moment the purchase of the new house we were moving to fell foul, leaving Chris and me virtually homeless.

I contacted Basildon Council and asked if it would be possible for them to re-house us temporarily, just until I could sort out the legal gaffe over the house I was moving to. Chris had suffered a heart attack recently, which did not help matters. I was quite prepared to sign a document to the effect that I would only require council accommodation until I could move into the new place. The council felt there was no reason why they should refuse. The manager of the BDC was prepared to use his influence with my building society to help. Then Tinworth and Potter stepped in and decided it should not happen. They knew it was a real emergency, but they had the council decision overturned, influencing others on the basis that I was an owner-occupier. This incident showed these pair in their true colours. If this was not vendetta, then I'm a Dutchman. Eileen Gelder was an owner-occupier, but did not prevent them from buying her home and giving her a council house.

The chairman of the BDC Board at the time was a man called Arthur Kelting; he was briefed to make peace between the Board and myself. As a result we got on very well and he was sympathetic to my plight. Accordingly, he offered me a corporation property to live in until I was able to move into my own house. As it transpired, Arthur Kelting was able to convince the building society that I should be allowed to move in straight away, and so I didn't have to take him up on his offer. As far as I was concerned relations between the Council and myself were at an all time low.

Even so, I was still rather sad at first when I finished with the council, but as time went by I was quite glad that I had left at the time I had. I missed the cut and thrust of the council chamber, but I had something none of the other councillors had: the respect of the people of Basildon.

Even away from the council, and outside of my social work, I still had to battle with authority at various times, either on my own behalf, or because I still tried to get justice for others. in 1979 my mother moved house to live with one of my sisters in Eastwood. She was now 86 and blind but the DHSS stopped her £20 a week supplementary benefit, as she had not told them she was moving until she went to live with her daughter. The DHSS office at Southend said they would have to visit her to sort the matter out, but could not do so for a while. In the meantime Mum had to live without her benefit. I kicked up a fuss, accusing the Southend office of incompetence and rudeness in a local press article. They were round to see Mum like a shot and pay her the money she was entitled to. That was the last thing I could do for Mum, she died not long afterwards.

For years after the Ugandan Asian business, people still used to think I was on the council. They still called me up at all hours with their grievances. Come to that, they still do to this day. I try not to disappoint them. I will still move heaven and earth to help anybody, particularly over housing matters. I could run a regular surgery with all the queries I get. Even some of the council officials called me 'councillor' for ages after I quit. People are always coming up to me in the street and market, stopping me with 'we need more people like you, Joe, why don't you go back on the council?' to which I just smile and say 'no, I done my share for this town'.

This town. I'm sad to see the way it has gone — it is just too big and impersonal now. Most of the councillors in office do their best, but increasingly they have come to be more concerned with their allowances than the people.

I wanted the town to be a success as a regional centre, with a life and vitality in the heart of it: plenty of places in the centre for young people — the lifeblood of all communities — to go and hang out and enjoy themselves, rather than be left on soulless estates with little prospect of work — the path to criminality for so many. My idea of Basildon would have been a community with community events and an environment that would nurture families, not tear them apart.

Instead we have a grey, impersonal monolith, the town centre, which is locked at nights like a medieval castle, except it is to keep the people out, rather than to take them in.

My old enemies at the BDC changed name and became the Commission for New Towns (CNT), but not a lot changed. It is supposed to be winding down all the old BDC functions, and the Government have said that power can pass to the local authority, if the council wins a ballot to be held to determine who will take over the CNT's housing stock. All this could have been done ten years ago, but of course, Basildon had a Labour council, and Thatcher would not have wanted any chance of them gaining such power.

The rules for this ballot are, as might be expected, farcical. The CNT makes up these rules, which state that all CNT properties will have one vote to cast for the council or against it. Anybody who does not vote will be deemed to have voted against the council, and the CNT will assume the votes of all empty properties; so no prizes for guessing how those votes would be cast. And it is not enough for the council to win the vote by a simple majority, or even a reasonable two-thirds majority, no, for the vote to be binding in their favour, the council would have to secure a 92 percent share of the vote.

From this it can be seen that the Government does not really want the council to take charge of and do as it pleases with the CNT housing stock. They would rather it went to a private housing association, which would not be a disaster in itself, but I can guarantee the terms imposed by such landlords would not square with those that a council inspired co-operative could offer.

In later years Tinworth resigned as leader, and made Peter Ballard 'boss' in his place. Ballard was a weak man, so Tinworth was still able to run things through his sidekick, Potter. Strange how history repeats itself.

Councillors continued to set up the most extraordinary financial deals, like those involving the Basco Company, which handled a contract to build a 'sportsdrome', worth millions, which George Walker, the since discredited head of the Brent Walker Group, got mixed up in. A million pounds was wasted on a plot of land that now lies unused. Potter and Tinworth managed to baffle the other councillors with figures, and a deal with some Irish banks went on to be an absolute financial disaster. Short term loans at huge interest rates were costing two and a half million pounds in repayments by 1991-2.

Money was thrown around like water in some areas, but grudgingly doled out elsewhere. At one meeting £138 thousand was thrown at the theatre which the Tories have since closed in line with spending cutbacks. Yet on the same night a bus service for the elderly and handicapped was scrapped. They will deny it if you asked them, or try to bamboozle you with all sorts of arguments, but the people of Basildon's money was wasted.

Another example of the sort of waste that became an easy target for the Tories was the 'women's drop-in' centres, which were supposed to provide support and social contact for the younger women on the housing estates. As a male chauvinist, I am naturally suspicious of anything strictly woman orientated — I preferred to call them 'drop-out' centres. So it proved, and they became a centre for all manner of activities, other than that for which they were intended.

It was no surprise when they were put on the chopping list brought about by central government's attempts to squeeze spending. I attended a meeting over proposed cuts at which a couple of women who ran one of these centres were protesting by holding up a banner and chanting. I looked at them and realised from my days in social work that one I knew to be a prostitute, and had put glass in a woman's face, leaving injuries which required 28 stitches. Were these and other council appointees fit to do their duties? The Tories lapped all this stupidity up.

My more sound pre-1973 plans were shelved. Basildon had no town hall, so I had proposed that a builder would construct a rent/lease town hall. The council would have paid a rent of £100,000 per annum for 25 years, when it would then own the building. The new Labour group decided they would build their own for £28 million. You do not need a maths degree to work out whose plan was cheaper.

The CNT has been just as happy to waste money — though in their case it is the taxpayer's cash that is abused. During the late 'eighties and early 'nineties, their sole concern seems to have been selling off land that could have been used in the public interest to private developers, whilst retaining their own big offices and large staff. Their building programme has consisted solely of houses, completely ignoring the need to attract industry with purpose-built units. To top it all, in the early 'nineties they managed to double the rents of the shops and industrial units that the BDC put up, leaving much of Basildon, particularly the centre, a proverbial ghost town.

I reported the CNT to their masters, the Department of the Environment about contracts that ex-CNT employees were mysteriously being awarded. The D.O.E. ignored me initially, so I wrote to the head of the civil service, care of the prime minister's office about their treatment of me. A senior official of the D.O.E. was soon on the line to me, 'don't write to the civil service head again, always ring me'. So I pressed home my case about contracts at the CNT.

Not only were perfectly good pavements being dug up and re-laid at great expense by the CNT's contractors, but the work on building a multi-million pound roundabout in the town centre was also given to the same firm, which was run by former engineers of the CNT. These men denied claims that they were still on the CNT's payroll, saying they had left their employment six months previously. Yet all the planning work had been on the books for three or four years prior to their departure.

I asked if it was true that they had effectively given the contracts to themselves. I was told by the CNT that the Ministry had allowed this state of affairs. Anyone made redundant by the CNT could be offered the contract work that they had been involved with at the

Commission. I promised that there would be questions in the House and a fraud investigation by the D.O.E., as I thought the whole thing a national disgrace.

The D.O.E. then told me that the CNT had got their facts wrong, because the department had ruled that work could be given, but not to the extent it was being doled out in Basildon. I was still not happy, so I wrote to the Shadow Minister for the Environment, since I knew the Tory Government would only try to obstruct me.

This time it was the D.O.E. who telephoned me.

'The Department wishes to thank you for the terrible mistake you have uncovered. We ruled three months work could be given to ex-employees, and there was a slip-up in communications — the CNT thought it was three years. We are taking away some of the contracts that have not been started yet, and the company concerned with have to tender for them.'

I gave my considered reply.

'I've never heard so much balls in my life. You are corrupt from top to bottom. Al Capone should have got the Nobel Prize compared to you lot.

All the official could respond with was, 'Be careful what you say'.

'What, would you send a hit-man after me, would you? With an umbrella with a poisoned tip?

At this point there was embarrassed laughter at the other end of the line, before an apologetic voice admitted, 'well, we have heard about you'.

The D.O.E. had heard of me alright, people know Joe Morgan, whether they are for him or against him, which is more than can be said for the current crop of councillors. People just do not even know their councillors any more. That has been the failing of the Labour Party in recent years. They have moved away from the ideas and the lives of the people they rely on to stay in office. They got away with it for a while in Basildon, and continued to rule the council. The days of councillors like George Elder, Mick Crew and even John Costello walking round town on a Sunday morning asking people what complaints they had and actually doing something about it, are long gone.

Even Tory victories in the parliamentary seat and the defection of a disillusioned Eric Moonman did not seem to be a big enough hint. So they shot themselves in the foot and effectively lied to the electorate, thinking they could treat them like idiots, but they underestimated the intelligence of the voters.

The Labour council tried to tell their poll tax payers that the reason for the high charge was all the fault of the Tory-controlled county council. This was not strictly true, but they decided it was a simple tale that they could tell to simple folk. The simple folk saw through them straight away. Not only did Labour snatch defeat from the jaws of victory at the 1992 general election, but the Labour group on the council was absolutely crushed by the Tories in the local votes. They refused to believe that the strategy was wrong. They just did not understand basic tenets of psychology, they only understood marketing and image.

I am afraid the difficulty with Basildon Labour Party accepting the blame for its woes is that it is a bit like an alcoholic admitting he has a drink problem — it is difficult to do, so they do not do it. At an inquest into the defeats, I said the main problem was that there were too many immigrants from the Tory Party. 'Rubbish,' was all that members could say, but that was the other main reason Labour lost.

I, on the other hand, have made a study of social psychology, both in the classroom and first hand, as a member of Essex's social workers team. I had left my insurance agent's job and taken up my greatest challenge — to try and help those who slip through the large holes in the net that we create in the fabric of modern living. It was harrowing and bleak at times, but it was the best job I have ever had, Leader of the Council included.

I was blessed in having worked for two very able men. The first was Don Glenn. He was a character himself. A big, brawny ex-lorry driver who had worked his way into becoming social work area chief, and in fact left to become Director of Social Services. He had more knowledge and common sense than the rest of England's university-trained directors of social work. He was immensely loyal to staff and would not let anyone attack them. He had his favourites and made those he did not like, know it. He helped me immensely and influenced my attitudes to social work.

Later David Holroyd became my boss, and although a Tory in outlook, he was also very supportive of me. Which was just as well when a well-known leading Labour councillor twice tried to have me disciplined for not doing my job correctly. In both cases he was proved wrong and was told so by David. In fact, both cases involved women this councillor was seeing privately. In one case the woman who complained that I had acted incorrectly in refusing to allow her to care an elderly man's monies and jewellery was a council worker. I had removed the chap to a psychiatric hospital and I had insisted the monies be put in a Social Services safe. The woman went to the councillor and claimed I had been insulting. One can only guess why she was so friendly with him, but David stuck up for me, said I was 100 percent correct in my action. Six months later the woman who was voluntary warden was dismissed by the council from her position for malpractice, there was talk of money missing again — was the councillor red-faced.

On the other occasion I took away into care the children of a woman, who coincidentally was having an affair with a Councillor. He complained, but my actions were upheld, and as a rank Tory, David really enjoyed writing to this councillor to ask for an apology.

A certain headmistress of a large school in Wickford was acting very snootily towards me at a meeting regarding one of her pupils who I was considering taking a place of safety order on for her own protection.

I deliberately emphasised the word 'headmistress' each time I addressed her. She wrote an official complaint to the director of social services, and my boss was asked to investigate — we convened a meeting, and Don Glenn innocently asked her what her pupils called her, she replied immediately.

'Headmistress, of course.'

'I see,' said Don Glenn, 'well now, what is your complaint against Mr Morgan...oh I see he called you "headmistress"?'

'Yes but it was the way he said it.'

'What was was that?'

'It had no respect in it.'

'Did you say 'headmistress' with no respect?' he asked me.

'I don't know,' I replied, 'how do you say "headmistress" with no respect?' I innocently asked.

This cunning banter went on for about 15 minutes and then Don said, 'Well headmistress, I think you owe Mr Morgan an apology for the accusations you made against him, especially as some fool in my office showed him your letter and so he could go to his solicitor.'

The woman looked shocked. 'No,' I intervened, 'I would never do that "HEADMISTRESS", I'm sure you are sorry about the whole episode.'

'Yes,' she replied.

Outside Don and I burst out laughing.

Social work became second nature to me, not only did it fill the large gap that council work left but it opened a new door that showed me life that no-one knows or wants to know about — social workers are the public sweepers, they are expected by the public to keep all the gory details of child abuse out of sight, they are expected to cope with all the problems of marital strife, mental illness, elderly, handicapped and all the intricate details of legislation, and if anything goes wrong the blame is all theirs — they are expected to be legal, medical, counselling and handyman experts, to cope with every known emergency — I entered social work not even aware of the complex situations that occur, and my reputation of being anti-authority and anti stupidity where local government officers were concerned was well-known, and militated against me to start with, though I was ignorant of the ill-feeling my arrival caused. Apparently some had reason to fear me being on the inside — but on the whole I was welcomed, and in time became respected, and if I say so myself, held in affection by the majority.

Of course, I created ill-feelings, especially amongst the lady bountiful and the social workers who made no attempt to understand the people they were serving, treating them as a nuisance and creating a them-and-us atmosphere.

I never remained quiet at staff meetings, being outspoken and caustic towards these sorts, but in the main most were people trying hard with a little help from chief officers of councillors to keep the less fortunate in society safe and secure. It always seemed to me that the type of social worker who had a true feel for the job was always pushed away by top management, but the worker who was in for a career and had no real understanding of people's expectations were often the ones promoted or listened to, perhaps it is due to social work being in the main a middle class profession and attracts a lot of people who have more problems than the clients they are supposedly helping.

At first I found the necessary full-time training very hard. I had to travel up to London to attend a board near the House of Lords, run by the blind and deaf, which was financed by the Government and the Royal National Institute for the Blind. For nine months I shuttled back and forwards on the railway between there and Basildon. I was not a young man any more. My angina finally forced me to retire two years early at 63. But between then and that first training, I can honestly say that I never wanted to go on holiday, such was the challenge and pull of the work.

And in nearly 20 years of social work I made many friends, even though, or perhaps because, I made no attempt to hide my politics or my colourful language to colleagues or clients; especially when I was called on to assess child abuse in cases where the child had to be removed, where I made it quite clear what I thought about the parents to their faces. This often led to my bosses pulling their hair, but in the end they accepted my way-out ways, and I became the longest serving worker in the department, staying there until my retirement. I rose up the pay scale rapidly, some would have said too rapidly. Strangely enough, clients not only accepted my attitude, they often specifically asked for me when needing help. Eventually the Chief Officers began to consult me on difficult cases.

One such concerned the parents of a blind girl suing the council over refusing to help send their daughter to a special school. I was asked to investigate the case, and re-examine the findings of the officers from social services involved. I reported back that although the officers had acted legally and correctly, I felt their decision was wrong. I discovered she was experiencing special problems due to profound deafness, and managed to 'talk' to her by using the sign language I had learnt on her hands. I felt she would benefit from attending the school, and that the council should make provision to help with the fees. The council accepted my findings and the parents dropped the case.

In my last 7 years I became an approved social worker under the Mental Health Act, this allowed me (with a second signatory), to compulsorily remove a person to psychiatric care if they were a danger to themselves or others. This left one always searching within, agonizing as to whether the decision taken was the right one.

Although it was very stressful work, it also had its bizarre and funny side. Perhaps people might have thought it callous when the people in my department joked about cases and actions, but in my opinion this was the safety valve that if not released would lead to a gamut of breakdowns amongst social workers.

One such case was when I had been threatened with a shotgun when taking some children away from a caravan they were living in to a place of safety. My senior, David Nichols, decided we would ask the police to organise assistance to secure the children. They agreed. We rendezvoused at the edge of the field where the caravan stood on a cold, foggy night. About half-a-dozen policemen, David and myself stealthily made our way, in a line, towards the caravan. All 5 foot 3 inches of me was sandwiched between a couple of six foot officers. I could hear myself breathing heavily. Suddenly the caravan door opened, a small dog leapt out, barking ferociously. My two escorts froze, then grabbed hold of me, terrified, which made three of us. Our whole operation was being held at bay by a tiny, yapping bundle of fur.

Then the two children came out of the caravan, each with a small bag pressed into their hands by their father, who shouted, 'You want them, you can have them'. With this the two children, six and eight years old, turned to the dog, a terrier, and said, 'Go in you naughty dog, you're frightening the nice policemen'. The dog tamely went away as some very red-faced adults, two of whom just had convulsions of laughter coming on, were led back to the cars by two small children.

On a more sustained farcical note, I was called out to hospitalize a manic West Indian woman — not the stuff of levity you might

168

think, but the sights and sounds that followed my entrance to her house could not but make me laugh afterwards.

When I arrived she was lying on the floor, naked underneath a sheet. She was obsessed with God and his counterpart down below. I walked in, and guess which side she thought I was on? Perhaps she had been talking to the Tory and Labour councillors at Basildon, but in any case, I was definitely an emissary from Old Nick. In my tow was a female colleague who was very good at her job. All the West Indian woman cared about was my colleague's jet black hair, which branded her a witch, I know, because she told us several times from underneath the sheet, which she now thought could protect her if she pulled it up far enough over her head — the old principle of 'if I can't see you, you can't see me'.

Then we were joined in our 'coven' by an Asian doctor whose grasp of the English tongue was limited, and what he was able to say came out in a Peter Sellers sing song voice. It transpired he did not understand the mental health act, so I explained to him what he should be diagnosing and what the legal requirements of him were. There was nothing new in this, as the majority of G.P.s tended to leave the diagnosis to the social worker approved under the terms of the act.

As I was explaining the ins and outs of the doctor's duties to him, the client pulled her sheet away and shouted at the G.P., 'You are after my pussy'.

The G.P. became very upset at this, and shouted back in his Peter Sellers voice, 'I do not want your pussy, I have one at home, why do I want yours, you stupid woman'.

He became more and more agitated as the client continued to play peek-a-boo with him, pulling the sheet over herself and then pulling it away. This was all too much for we pair of social workers, and we collapsed in laughter, which so enraged the doctor that he signed the form and stormed out, still shouting, 'I do not want your min, I have one in my wife at home'.

For quite a few years after this episode I had other occasions when it was necessary to compel this woman to go to hospital. If as I led her through the corridors we would sometimes pass my female colleague, the woman would push herself against the wall farthest away from us and make the sign of the cross, mumbling about the devil's witch as my colleague passed by.

In another rather complex and nasty case, I had supported a young woman who wanted to deny access to her child by the father, a rather obnoxious and wealthy man who had some pull with my bosses. He tried everything to make me drop my support for denial of access, even to the point of deliberately arranging that legal

169

advice would be held from me, knowing that I would be spending a whole day in the witness box in the high court when the matter came before a judge.

The day of the case arrived, the father's barrister produced an affidavit to the effect that the social worker (me), had arrived at the father's house dressed in scruffy clothes, with a long hairstyle and carrying a copy of the 'Daily Worker' — in short, a typical, woolly-minded social worker, unfit to be involved in the case. I turned to the bench and told the judge that I only wished the barrister was right about my long hair (I was nearly bald by then). The court, including the judge, erupted in laughter, the barrister was on a losing streak after that little fabrication.

But life was not without danger: when visiting manic clients on one occasion, my rough and ready background saved me from serious injury — I went to visit a heavily-built young man who had a severe personality disorder. He came out of his flat and grabbed me, then proceeded to do his damnedest to push me down the middle of the stair well, a 50-foot drop. I knew it was useless trying to reason with him, so my knee used its own forceful argument on his privates. He understandably screamed with pain, I understandably bolted. I wonder how some of my middle class colleagues would have fared — probably none too well, persisting as they surely would in using text-book reasoning even as they plummeted towards the ground.

When I reported my torn coat and the assault to the county chiefs, they predictably did not want to know. It all smacked of bad publicity as far as they were concerned, to hell with the social workers, the county image could not be tarnished by prosecuting a man with a mental problem. Out of all the senior officers in social services that I came across, only Don Glenn and David Holroyd gave a damn about their people on the front line, and that because they had both attended the same academy as myself — the academy of real life.

Yet just when you thought that the job was all earnest efforts to combat child abuse, mental cruelty and hardship, something would come along to counter-balance all that, and make even the most cynical person (yes, that's me) smile. There can be no greater feeling of job satisfaction in the world than to have young people you helped some five or ten years previously coming back to thank you, or reading letters from the grateful relatives of the elderly that you gave years of care and attention to.

The dedicated social workers do outnumber the purely career advancement and county set, and do their very best in difficult circumstances, and thank goodness for that. It was the most stressful job I ever had, but I loved it and would not have swapped it for anything else. Most importantly of all, it kept me in touch with the people, something I could have easily missed out on after leaving the council in 1972.

Now in my later years, I have become a little more mellow and reflective. I have the time to think about the world around us in a more considered manner. But every time I do, I seem to find that my old suspicions and fears, often based on anger and instinct, were invariably right.

For instance, Thatcher succeeded in smashing the unions, but where did it all start? Barbara Castle, that is where. If she had not brought out her ideas for curtailing the unions in her paper 'In place of strife'. then the Tories would probably never embarked on the road that started with Ted Heath and the miners and ended with Thatcher breaking Scargill's coal strike. I notice some Tory M.P.s were genuinely concerned about the plight of the miners when plans were announced in the autumn of 1992 to axe 31 pits. Sorry lads, too little, too late. And for those of you with mining constituencies, I think the tears were either crocodile ones or spilt for yourselves when you thought about the prospect of defending that vicious policy at the ballot box.

The NHS is a similar story, Ted Heath might have started tinkering with it by introducing his administration reforms, but it was Labour that really stuck the knife in and twisted it by beginning prescription charges. It is not too surprising that the Tories have continued to raise them ever since, given the example of the 'People's Party'. that claimed to be the champion of free health care.

Labour could still win with the old ideals of the 'twenties and 'thirties if they sensibly updated them to the twenty-first century, rather than the headlong dash to become a mark two SDP. Nationalisation could still work for major industries and public utilities. It is about time that the banks were brought under state control too, free market forces in banking have brought nothing but misery for business and ordinary borrowers and savers alike.

I am an advocate of selling off council houses, unlike many of my fellow Labour Party members. After all, the idea of socialism is to make people as free and affluent as possible. Home owning is freedom coupled with affluence IF tackled in the right way, that is, not the Tory inspired state of things where people on low wages become slaves to mortgages or the threat of repossession. The most sensible way to go about this is through co-operatives — a good old socialist idea — all British councils should form their housing stock into co-operatives and say 'we have no more housing'. People could part own or rent at advantageous terms. The idea has flexibility and security.

Small industry could likewise benefit from co-operatives, as it did so well in the socialist Spain of the 1980s. People's resources are

171

being vastly under-employed in this country, by clubbing together they could increase their efficiency without having to rely so heavily on the banks for capital expansion.

Something else that Basildon, with its ideal geographical position in particular could have benefited from was a more whole-hearted approach to Europe. We have so many common interests with all the other European nations, particularly peace and prosperity, that it is galling to see people hanging back from putting Britain in the heart of things because of long memories and a few worries about the mass of red-tape and stupid edicts that Brussels spouts out. We should swear ourselves to the idea of a united Europe, and then sort out all the bureaucratic stupidity from inside, not throw stones like spoilt kids from outside. M.P.s worry about loss of sovereignty, but they mean their sovereignty, not that of the people. We should fight for the sort of Europe we want, not whine about the one we have.

Even if a Labour government were returned tomorrow, it would be the same old story; they would retain most of the legislation that the Tories have used to strip this nation of its Welfare State, the most disgusting aspect of all their greed-motivated policies. I have warned Labour Party members that they have got to fight to ensure that a future labour government puts back what the Tories have removed; they must not take it for granted that it will happen, because it will not. Labour ministers betrayed this country before, and could do again, unless they are clear about their commitment to this country's welfare.

The 1990's leaders of the Labour Party at national level seem to have been cut from the same cloth that most of Wilson's ministers were made of. It is quite easy to imagine John Smith, Margaret Beckett and Gordon Brown all becoming creatures of HM Treasury, bowing to the jealous civil service, which believes it has all the answers, and that the politicians and the people are fools for daring to think otherwise. Not that Neil Kinnock would have been any better.

I first met Kinnock when he was a young M.P. in the House of Commons. Eric Moonman introduced him to me in the restaurant there. (At one stage during the last Labour government I spent as much time there as I did at Basildon; I knew most of the Labour members by their first names.) We sat and discussed housing matters, particularly with reference to the New Towns for a while, and so we shook hands and parted amicably enough.

Kinnock was a user and a shape changer, that is how he got to the top, on other people's backs and other people's clothes. He was not without talent, but he was far too concerned with image, he thought he could copy Tory successes in that department, but he failed to

172

realise that substance was more important. He preferred to surround himself with people like Peter Mendelssohn, the nephew of Herbert Morrison, who painted a fantastic rosy coloured picture of everything. Everybody agrees Kinnock had good personal election campaigns, but Labour still finished second, which in the first past the post electoral system really is nowhere. I expect he will end up doing what life made him for — appearing as a pundit on anything and everything on television.

On a more local note, I have come to be looked on as a sort of elder statesman in the local party — very much 'Father Joe' — without the snide Stalinist implications it had when used by my enemies.

I enjoy being the father figure. Of course, I realise that young people in the Party have their own ways and their own views, but it is nice when they listen and ask for advice.

Above all, any servant of the public, be he councillor or cabinet minister, must accept that they are accountable. That was always my tenet in power, and it remains so now.

Chris and I have lived in a bungalow since 1988. In my council days I was all for making separate housing provision for old people, but first hand experience has convinced me I was wrong. There is a lack of independence, as power-mad wardens patrol up and down outside, warding off children who walk through and anyone else they think 'unsuitable' — that is, anyone who might give the place a bit of life. My view now is that old people should be integrated into housing plans, but still given the ability to summon help if necessary. That way they can remain part of the community, rather than living a life excluded from family and friends. Chris and I are lucky in that we still get to see our family. My son, Harry and I are not as close as I am to my grandchildren, but he is proud of what I have achieved, and puts up with me jibing at him as a chequebook socialist.

And if anyone out there thinks old Joe Morgan is going to quietly slip into his dotage, then they had better watch out.

I still go to ward meetings and speak my mind. Harold Wilson might have dumped 'Victory for Socialism' once it had served its purpose for him, but you never know, 'Father Joe' has still got some fire in his belly, so he just might revive the movement one day soon and once again manage to upset a few people....

* * *

I had been lying in bed for some time by now, the rain was still working hard on the window pane. So many thoughts had gone through my mind.

173

Then Chris woke up and chided me,

'Are you going to get up and make some breakfast, or are you waiting for me to get up?'

I smiled. I leant across and cuddled her. 'I'll make breakfast love, you stay in bed if you want.'

As I shuffled across to the bathroom the telephone rang, I answered it. It was the grandchildren.

'You just got up, Grandad?'

'No, I've been up a long while darlings.'

'What you been doing?'

'Well, I've been writing my life story so that you can read it one day.'

Laughter from several loving people down the line.

'Writing your life story while you was in bed?'

'Well, I started it.'

'Make sure you put in all those stories you told us Grandad, the true stories and the untrue ones.'

'All the stories I've been thinking about are true. Perhaps one day I'll get round to writing the fairy-tale side just for you children. But you know them all, that's the important part. I'll pick you up later.'

I traipsed back to see Chris, told her who had been on the 'phone, and the conversation that had passed. She said they would be too frightened to print a book of my life, I agreed, and then added,

'But as I've said before, put them all together, all the notables, all the Royalty and top politicians I've met, and none of them are worth a toss. They were all out to line their own pockets and look after themselves. The only real friends the working class of this country ever had were their own work mates, and above all, their own families.'

I went back to the bathroom and cleaned my teeth, then began to shave. As I looked at the face half-covered in foam regarding me from the mirror, I grinned a private grin, and burst into song, with my own version of 'The Red Flag':

'The working class can kick my arse,

I'm a Member of Parliament at last....